LAST NIGHTS OF PARIS

Last Nights of Paris

by
Philippe Soupault

translated by
William Carlos Williams

SOUPA

EXACT CHANGE CAMBRIDGE

1992

© 1928 Philippe Soupault
Originally published in French as *Les Dernières Nuits de Paris*
Translation © 1982 the estate of Florence Williams
Afterword © 1982 Full Court Press

This edition © 1992 Exact Change
Published by arrangement with Renée Soupault,
New Directions, and Ron Padgett

Quotation from *Paterson* © 1958 W.C. Williams
Reprinted by permission of New Directions

All Rights Reserved
ISBN 1-878972-05-7

Photograph by Hilde Rantzsch, "Portrait" (1927)
Reproduced by permission of The MIT Press

Exact Change books are edited by Damon Krukowski
and designed by Naomi Yang

Exact Change
P.O. Box 544
Cambridge, MA 02139
USA

Co-author with André Breton of the first self-proclaimed book of automatic writing, *Les Champs Magnétiques* (1919), and co-editor with Breton and Louis Aragon of the avant-garde journal *Littérature* (1919–1923), Philippe Soupault was one of the founders of the Surrealist movement. A poet, novelist, and journalist, with a much less political and less theoretical approach to writing than his colleagues Breton and Aragon, Soupault was expelled from the movement in 1926—along with Antonin Artaud—for "their *isolated* pursuit of the stupid literary adventure." *Les Dernièrs Nuits de Paris* was his third prose work, published in 1928.

Last Nights of Paris in English is a surprising artifact of the twenties. Written by one of the founders of Surrealism and translated by William Carlos Williams, it stands at the unlikely juncture of both French and American literary modernism. As the many memoirs of Paris in the twenties attest, the disparate worlds of the French avant-garde and the American expatriates rarely collided (a few famous fist fights and other café antics aside). However Soupault was by many accounts unusually interested in the Americans (he wrote the foreword to a French translation of Nathanael West's *Miss Lonelyhearts,* for example); and Williams, as Soupault himself recounts in the afterword to this edition, kept his distance from the expatriates while in Paris and welcomed an introduction to the French writer by their mutual friend, the American editor Matthew Josephson. The result was this novel's English translation, which Josephson published for Macaulay and Co., New York, in 1929.

Indeed, *Last Nights of Paris* seems to share much with both the Surrealist novels *(Nadja, Paris Peasant)* and the American expatriate novels *(The Great Gatsby, The Day of the Locust)* of its day. Its underworld setting, the narrator's obsession with a woman and identification of her with the place she inhabits, the plot that seems to tend toward con-

flagration, its preoccupation with chance and with the city—
all could be drawn variously from the novels mentioned
above. Perhaps *Last Nights of Paris* points to some shared
concerns of those mutually exclusive café societies; or per-
haps the book simply captures the mood of Paris in the
twenties as it appeared to both its native writers, and to
those who came from across the Atlantic; the Paris which
was the site for the romantic genesis of both French and
American modernism, which coincide however briefly in
Williams' translation of Soupault's "Dadaist novel".

What has happened
                    since Soupault gave him the novel
                              the Dadaist novel
to translate—
                    The Last Nights of Paris.
                              "What has happened to Paris
since that time?
                    and to myself"?

                    A WORLD OF ART
          THAT THROUGH THE YEARS HAS

                              SURVIVED!

                    —*William Carlos Williams,* PATERSON

CHAPTER ONE

Choosing is Aging.

She smiled so curiously I could not keep my eyes from her pale face, and it may be that in spite of myself I answered her smile as one would a mirror. Naturally—indeed it was quite the most natural thing in the world—she was drinking a *menthe verte*, since in this city all those whose profession is love make no secret of their devotion to this odd beverage which is nothing but a liquid candy. The café was taking a little nap. The aperitif hour had passed, and that of chocolate and sandwiches had not yet come. The waiters stood about with bowed heads and dangling arms. A few had seated themselves, looking much like those statues that receive gold medals at the salon and adorn public squares—useless, motionless and out of date.

A light breeze stirred from time to time, weaving a tranquil and monotonous design.

She stood up and I, likewise; I walked beside her along the boulevard Saint-Germain and in front of the booth of the anti-alcoholic league, which still displayed its dried brains, I said to her:

"Evidently it would be best to cross over."

"As you please."

And we crossed the boulevard, turning our backs on anti-alcoholism.

Hearts throbbed in the trees; it was the end of summer and someone leaning on his elbows in a window said to the night: "It is cold." . . . Possibly, thought I, but one thing at a time.

A little bell like that of a church wakened the lights and gave an acid sharpness to the billboard of Saint-Germain-des-Prés. Signs were made. By whom, to whom? Briefly, it was white night. The eleven o'clock mist. The little lady cooed and mumbled alternately in the manner of one who who powders, and then rouges her lips. The same care, the same coquetry. She led me to the boulevard Saint-Michel, then round the Luxembourg, eyes closed.

Dogs were running about in this beautiful senatorial enclosure, now filled with immense shadows. I lent my ears to the uproar. A sort of fountain pronounced a couplet, the stupid refrain of the Latin Quarter, a ten cent song which the students sing in order to get the name of students: berets, caps, flowing ties.

"Have you noticed," said my snowy companion, "that in this fool park there is never a butterfly?"

A big dog—prisoner or jailer, who knows?—barked loudly.

The rue de Medicis along which we were strolling at a fair pace is sad around ten-thirty at night. It is the street of everlasting rain.

It is said that along one side of it is the meeting place of masochistic bachelors. A modest and silent club. Here umbrellas take on the appearance of a flock.

"You know," she said, "that around here are places where you can get coffee with cream."

At its very start the rue de Vaugirard stinks of books. The odor comes from every side. Its friend and neighbor, the rue de Tournon, is more inviting. So much so that I was prepared for a proposal and the address of a comfortable hotel.

At night, the Senate building looks like absolutely nothing. One sees only a great disc which roars in a bass voice: *Ralentir*—slow down—which, it is said, the nearsighted misread regularly, thinking it to be *Repentir*.

The virtuosity of words in this historic quarter is amazing. Those that escape from the houses have a quicksilver sheen, those that hide in their cracks are phosphorescent.

She who proposed nothing reminded me that because of them the rue de Tournon was indiscreet.

"Quite so," said I. "Cold has no effect on the faces of streets."

"That's just a lot of blah."

I did not insist.

We came out upon the carrefour de Buci, a crossroads which gives birth to a family of short narrow streets, not alleys but dark and full of bad smells.

The lights of a small café splashed with syrup the triangular and morose façades of nameless shops.

In that rue de Seine, which still wonders at its own existence, we chanced on a meeting which can be described neither as pleasant, shocking nor inclined to destroy one's peace of mind, but which left a shadowy trace, a streak of black across the landscape of our evening. A black dog, a poodle, a watchdog no doubt, was running zigzag from one side of the street to the other as if he had lost his mind. Neither the hour nor the bad weather seemed to slow the comings and goings of this pariah pup. I felt sure that he was waiting for us. He did not have the look, though, of a dog bent on mischief. When he caught sight of my companion, he seemed to recognize her and circled about her, barking. I don't know whether she recognized him or not because first she said: "Hush, dog," and then added: "What's the meaning of this beast, anyway?"

We continued our walk which grew ever more monotonous. A few drops began to fall. It was a veritable downpour. At once we hurried our steps and took refuge in the draft of air which blows perpetually through the vaulted passageway leading from the rue de Seine to the quay, and loses itself in the Institute.

The dog followed us at a trot, now passing us, now stopping, showing by this that he had made up his mind to follow us to the ends of the earth.

First we listened to the falling rain, breaking the monotony of this song by no less monotonous comments about the rain.

"What rotten weather!"

"What rotten weather!"

"Good God, what weather!"

The dog lay quietly at our feet. Now and again a taxi passed full tilt and my psst! just made it double its pace.

"Would you like me to tell you my name?"

The dog replied: "Yes,"—that is, he gave a short bark.

"My name is Georgette."

There's an astounding name, makes one think of a needle, a hem, a spot of grease. This name without beginning, or end, calls to mind the grandeur of thrones, or the moon in a mist.

To utter that name is enough to bring back the memory of a toothache or a couple of good smacks in the face.

I kept these reflections to myself, being content to summarize them under the simple adjective which says, by the way, a plenty:

"Charming."

I had scarcely finished the last syllable when the dog stood up and made himself pleasant by sticking out his tongue. Then the strangest events of that evening began to unfold.

The signal was given by the image of the Republic. A sudden wind followed the rain, a wind like a knife blade, a sort of squall that gathered a newspaper dragging along the pavement and placed it with one stroke in the hands of the statue posing in the square.

An open carriage passed in the rue de Seine. The horses were at full gallop but the driver brought them at top speed skillfully around the corner where the rue de Seine stops.

I had time to notice in the carriage an extremely pale person whom I took to be the former Police Commissioner, Lépine. The coachman whipped his horses, made two turns about the statue of Voltaire and stopped sharply before the entrance to the Bibliothèque Mazarine.

"Monsieur Lépine" stepped down. He was dressed in black and wore a high hat. I saw him disappear through the court of the Institute. The coachman jumped from his seat and began to unharness the horses.

The Republic dropped her paper. The wind drew off and moved toward the Pont-Neuf.

Some minutes passed. I offered Georgette a cigarette which she accepted. We had hardly finished lighting our Camels when we beheld a veritable cortège on the Pont des Arts. A dozen men dressed like laborers, broadly belted with red or blue flannel, were sadly carrying a long box. Back of them were young fellows in caps pushing lengthy handcarts containing planks and timbers.

When these people noticed the carriage and horses, they hurried forward and in their turn entered the courtyard of the Institute.

Dragging an umbrella as one drags along an unhappy cur, a couple passed on the quay and stopped an instant to cast a look around. I saw them take to their heels. The woman let out little shrieks that recalled those of a screech owl. They checked their umbrella on the steps of the Pont des Arts.

Hearing it strike midnight, the youthful Georgette naturally could not keep from shivering and I from saying, with a smile that followed a sneering laugh:

"The hour of crimes."

I acknowledge willingly that the time and the place were not well chosen for this classic pleasantry. The dog, which had remained quiet until then, felt impelled to sniff the trail of his fellows along the walls. Following him with my eyes, I happened upon a freshly posted ad. In the glimmer of the miserable lamp which lights the passageway after a fashion, I could make out words which seemed to flutter in the wind.

I could not finish reading because an auto, one of those usually spoken of as high-powered, crossed the Pont-Neuf with gleaming headlights and pulled up before the railing of the Institute. A large greyhound leaped from the car, followed by a man in a brown derby who at once commanded:

"Put out the lights."

A moment later, he called out:

"Domino?"

And he whom I had taken for M. Lépine answered the call. Both lifted their hats, but what surprised me was that they did not shake hands. They talked together for a minute or two and I understood by a gesture that the man in the brown derby was saying: "Go."

Lépine made haste forthwith to disappear and the man in the derby began to pace up and down before the railing. The rain now fell with redoubled violence and the lights of the last tram cast long running flames on the surface of the river.

Georgette, in a tragic voice, which, however, did not make me feel like laughing, proposed:

"Let's go."

But this night I understood the meaning of that well known journalistic cliché: to be riveted to the ground.

To keep my sang-froid, I had to content myself with recourse to recollections of all sorts.

The hygiene of fear.

Thus flows the Seine ever for those who are throttled by love, fear, religion or madness, those sentiments which are such powerful narcotics.

Near me a drama or what I thought to be a drama was taking place, and here this fatherly river was permitting spring or summer images to approach me: a steamer bedecked with flags, some swimmers whom I found really distressing, and the recollection of an evening I had spent leaning on the parapet of the Pont Marie watching several lifesavers trying in vain to recover the body of an unfortunate suicide.

All these pictures, of little moment perhaps, rose before my eyes which by now were adjusted to the darkness of the night, dressed in hues the warmest and most intense. Out of a kindly feeling I described them to the youthful Georgette who while listening to my talk grew more and more uneasy.

Soothed by my own words, distracted by the sound of my voice, I paid no further attention to the person who was persistently walking up and down, who seemed not to notice the scared trio that we made, Georgette, the dog and I.

But we had to quit that passageway and get on with our walk.

I suggested to my companion that we return on our tracks, but with the stubbornness of timid people and of loiterers, she refused and said:

"Have you no curiosity?"

I protested. But I did not say to her that I was afraid of witnessing a tragic scene or some strange act; I did not dare tell her that our presence at this hour, in this place, seemed to me absolutely inappropriate, even suspicious. Hanging upon my arm, Georgette kept looking and seemed impatient to discover the reason for the comings and goings of all these people. The dog, who had stretched himself out at our feet, raised himself on his forepaws, pricking up his ears. By this he called to our notice the arrival of a young man who came to shelter himself within the passage where we had taken refuge. The appearance of our new companion made no particular impression on me. His overcoat collar was turned up and his faded slouch hat was pulled down about his ears.

Without greeting of any sort, he asked us:

"Anything new?"

I did not hesitate to answer:

"No, nothing"—without taking into account that by so doing I accepted the rôle of an accomplice.

"They won't get him," he predicted. "I searched the three streets designated by Volpe and found nothing."

Having thus spoken, he drew off and leaned against the wall, showing by this that he had made up his mind to await indefinitely the sequel of events.

The dog, who in this mystery remained our sole guide, went to sniff the newcomer and came back to us to give us his verdict.

With hands in the pockets of his overcoat, the nonchalant young man seemed to be sleeping with open eyes. I was able to take him in at leisure. He had a thin pale face, a short blond moustache, a thick nose and faded blue eyes. His whole person had about it an air of anonymity which rendered him antipathetic. His unbrushed clothes, covered with ugly wrinkles, made me think of a servant out of employment and now more servile than ever. Further than that, I felt certain that he was an after-dark professional. His voice, which I had scarcely noticed, suddenly resounded in my memory magnified by the delay: it was a bass voice such as none but thin men own.

The long minutes—minutes of syrup—flowed into silence. An auto horn now and then broke the monotony. The dog seemed to sleep and to melt away into the shadows.

The man in a brown derby drew near our refuge and by the light of a street lamp I was able to make out his features. What struck me most was his nose, very long, and his very white teeth. Almost a false death's head.

At last he stopped and with a blast from a whistle summoned M. Lépine, who appeared. He seemed obsequious in the vile gaslight. Silently they waited, without a move.

"Isn't that you, Georgette?" suddenly remarked the pale young man.

"It took you long enough to recognize me," replied the young woman, most naturally. I turned with an angry look toward the last speaker. I wondered what could be the meaning of this disquieting dialogue and I scented I don't know what crooked business.

Quickly I made up my mind: raising my coat collar, I prepared to quit this determined couple, to leave them to their little game. A roll of drums, and my curiosity stopped me short. It was a muffled beat, choked back, as if the drummer feared to make too much noise.

"There they come," said Georgette.

And sure enough a procession was to be seen approaching,

led by the drum. Four men framed a woman with hanging hair, pale, a set smile on her lips, a smile of suffering. She carried a sort of bag in her arms.

They stopped before the statue of the Republic. The man in the brown hat, followed by M. Lépine, advanced toward the woman who fell at once to her knees.

I heard her crying. She raised her hands. The four men in derbies forced her to stand up and, preceded by the brown derby, shoved her into the court.

There was a scream, then I saw the woman come running out. She was quickly recaptured. Then with a disconsolate gesture she held the sack out to the man in the derby, accompanying the gift with a single word:

"Bastard!"

Then, vanquished, she let herself fall to the ground before the railings of the Institute. She lay motionless, almost in the gutter. No one thought to raise her.

One after another they drew off. The auto into which the man who held the sack had climbed set off at a great clip, then M. Lépine, then the drummer, then those who seemed to be laborers.

"See you soon," said my neighbor lifting his hat.

"Are you coming, Sweetie?" said Georgette to me.

"Oh, to hell with you."

Georgette, unmoved by my violence, waited meekly. I wanted to take a look at the woman lying motionless on the pavement. Georgette guessed my intention and gave me to understand:

"She'll get away all right by herself."

The tempest of silence. No longer a sound, no longer a glimmer. The darkness was profound.

She who seemed to sleep made not the slightest move and a calm fell upon her like a gentle and consoling snow.

The Parisian night had seized the square; and the black walls, the quays, the bridge vanished as if never to reappear. Long reflections waxed in the monotone of the sky, those colorless rainbows that betray the city and its dawn.

Played out, distressed, I had no idea what the next move should be. On the sidewalk, with outstretched arms, the woman seemed begging to be left alone. Georgette had disappeared without breathing a word, leaving me embarrassed and uneasy. Nothing made the night real for me. A strange indifference—a Parisian indifference to be exact—surrounded these last events. I had no wish to laugh or to move. By luck, a living thing, the dog, came up to me and forced me to shake off my lethargy.

I heard steps in the rue de Seine, heavy, almost familiar steps, and I rushed to announce the presence of that prostrate woman.

Without hastening his step (in recalling all this, I wondered later if he were not obeying a word of command) the officer, whom I came upon in the rue de Seine, wanted to know if I were all there. By which I concluded I must have looked badly frightened.

When we arrived at the place, the woman was gone. A taxi, at least I thought so, was just making off.

The officer shrugged his shoulders and out of habit gave me a shove as they do to drunkards to make them move on.

I moved on all right. At a good clip I followed the quays in the direction of the Gare d'Orsay.

O melancholy, melancholy, that night I understood your power and your slavery. On the banks of this river I seemed to be pursuing a flock of memories, regrets, and when at last I was about to seize one of these phantoms, I forgot, forgot forever, my mania or my despair. That woman, sorrowful to the point of death, was somewhere behind me, still waiting no doubt, and I cannot tell what fear drove me forward. I fled. The great clock of the Gare d'Orsay, the one on the left, pointed to three, strangest hour of all and comparable only to the mystic ninth.

The station was cold. I looked about in vain for a cheering drink. No trains were being announced and only a few lights still kept watch. But, as after an accident, the station seemed more deserted than the quays. Nobody was waiting for anyone. There was nothing left me, I thought, but to sing. Bad luck was following me. It was three o'clock, the hour of indecision. I heard noises on one of the stairs and saw a sailor come up carrying a great cylindrical sack of white canvas.

He approached me stumbling and raising his free hand to his béret asked me:

"Paris?"

He had an enormous head, red, and blond, the face of a strangler with thin lips and enormous brown hands.

"This is Paris."

"Thanks."

And stumbling, stumbling he moved off, then put down his sack and came back to me again.

"Got a cigarette?"

He chose one from the pack I offered him and without

saying a word lighted it from the one I held between my lips. I saw close to my face those enormous cheeks which alternately swelled out and collapsed as he drew in the smoke.

"Thanks," said he, then after a silence he added:

"It's night."

The dog, companion whom I had forgotten, came galloping into the station and ran over to us. He sniffed the sailor, then circling me and letting his tongue hang out one side of his mouth, he quietly seated himself facing the sailor.

"Your mutt?"

I said yes so as not to be forced to give an explanation and turned on my heel followed by the dog, already faithful.

But the sailor who probably did not know where to go at this footless hour, imitated the pup and, laden with his sack, followed us, hoping for another cigarette, some conversation, or just somewhere to go.

I would gladly have changed rôles, so impossible was it for me to shake off my torpor and decide finally upon a direction. I was expecting it to turn cold.

We passed before the Chambre des Députés, crossed the bridge and the place de la Concorde, always in Indian file.

I turned into the Champs-Elysées in the hope of encountering a familiar face. Some old custom dressed in the guise of a woman of the streets, one of the Champs-Elysées crowd who go in for certain special practices. They circle ceaselessly about the little clumps of shrubs and trees, as if they were arc lights or banknotes. Then I turned in the direction of the Petit Palais.

In the shadow of this building, which makes one think, by the way, of a skeleton, silent councils are held between midnight and 5:00 A.M. It is said that in certain of these corners a dozen women have been strangled since the year 1920. Thanks to mutual understandings, the police close their eyes and keep away from crimes of this nature which at no price should be made public. I thought the sailor would not escape these women who have other attractions than their beauty.

One of them, gliding rather than walking, approached our Indian file and by movements of the hands and eyes sought to attract our attention.

Seized with a sudden inspiration I stopped and asked in a low voice—the only tone which suited that place:

"Is Georgette here?"

For answer she was content to whistle thrice softly and from the shadows emerged a young woman whom I recognized to be her whom I had accompanied for a part of the evening.

As she was approaching our group, I said to myself that what I had taken for a sudden inspiration was only obedience to certain special habits which overrun Paris.

The dog recognized Georgette and barked joyfully, which had the direct effect of scaring the sailor who quickly backed up for a few steps.

"Where are we going?"

I expected that petulant and vicious question. It is the night's query and Georgette did no more than express aloud that eternal interrogation.

One more question without answer, a question one asks of the stars, the weather, the shadows, the entire city.

Georgette, the sailor, the dog and I myself had no answer ready and this we sought wandering at random, driven here rather than there by an invincible fatigue.

Thinking it over as we were walking with soft steps under the trees of the Champs-Élysées, I seemed to catch a purpose, that of all the night prowlers of Paris: we were in search of a corpse.

If all at once we had encountered a lifeless form lying prostrate on the pavement, bathed perhaps in his own blood, or propped against a wall, we should have come immediately to a halt and that night would have been ended. But it was that encounter, and that encounter only, which could have satisfied us.

I know, we know, that in Paris death alone has power to quench that pointless thirst, to bring to a close an aimless walk. A corpse confronts us with eternity.

O inviolable secret of Paris! A prostitute, a sailor, a dog, helped me that night to glimpse you.

Shadows, nothing but shadows, peopled the Champs-Elysées; impelled by them, groping, I sought the form of the secret.

It grew cold, then came a white glimmer like the crowing of a cock.

It was early dawn. I quickened my step.

Georgette, the sailor, and the dog disappeared, taking leave noiselessly.

Daybreak. Paris, heavy-headed, began to fall asleep.

CHAPTER TWO

Chance is but our ignorance of causes.

—Lamarck

It was not until the next day toward five that I learned from the evening papers a part of the truth and the rôle in a drama that I myself had involuntarily played.

I was seated outside a café on the Champs-Elysées before a "petit moka" when a poorly-clad old man in broken down patent leather shoes, a newsboy friend of mine, came up and, with a gracious smile, held out a paper saying, "A nice crime for you."

I read that they were on the assassin's track, a sailor from the Chacal who had killed and cut to pieces one of his friends. A commonplace crime, that's all, said I half aloud. I was disappointed; it so happened that at this time the discovery of bags full of limbs, carefully sawed off and chopped up, was an almost daily occurrence; they were found in various spots—in the Saint-Martin canal, or under the portal of a church, or in some ordinary entryway. What seemed especially remarkable was that, when an inventory was made, the heads or hands of the victims were regularly missing. They dragged the canals in vain, they searched the city with no more success. The head, the hands and the assassin were not to be found and the police were laying themselves out. Now and again, fairly regularly in fact, they would announce that they were on the track of the criminal, or it might be, the sadist; but shortly after, this trace was found to be false. The butcher or cook suspected victoriously proved his innocence.

The papers that evening stated with remarkable accuracy that they strongly suspected a sailor to be the murderer of the young man who had been cut to pieces and found in that state under the Pont-Neuf, and left it to be understood that it was in all probability not his first offense.

A woman, concubine of this sailor, had that very night, it seems, given him away within a few yards of the place where the dismembered body had been thrown.

I called to mind the strange scenes of which I had been a witness and quite naturally I made the persons I had happened upon the principal actors in the crime. The places, the time and the details given made me think I had some reason so to believe. To be less disturbed, I left the tables at Fouquet's and, pondering the whole matter, installed myself in a small deserted bar situated on the quay not far from the bridge over which the subway passed. Aided by the walk, I endeavored to tabulate my recollections and to live over again the preceding night. By a singular fancy which was perhaps a simple illusion, I persuaded myself little by little that I had witnessed this terrible betrayal in seeing the torture of that cursing woman and that in my presence she had given away the sailor, her lover. It was my ignorance, I told myself, that caused my amazement at all the show that had surrounded this treason, at all the pomp displayed on this occasion. I overlooked, doubtless, that the police are accustomed to these spectacular third degree methods and that the moral "inquisition" long since replaced mechanical means of forcing a confession.

I thought it over. I said to myself that in Paris in 1928 scenes of this sort are really impossible, that police plots of this sort are ridiculous, forgetting that I could not possibly know all the mysteries and all the intricacies of this city in which it was my habit to live. At this point in my reflections I pushed open the door of the little *bistro* kept by one of those chaps who specialize in the sale of firewood and coal for the home.

I sat down at a table, spread out my papers and called for a glass of *vin gris*.

Despite the noise on the quay, despite the periodic thunder of the metro and the rumble of passing trucks, I reread the reports about the crime and its betrayal.

Someone, as was customary in the place, had seated himself at my table.

"Remarkable," said he to me.

"Of what are you speaking?" I answered.

He started to chuckle, somewhat contemptuously:

"About the young fellow cut into chunks."

I always forget that understanding which springs up so readily between two men seated at the same table. He had read my thoughts which, after all, must have been perfectly clear. He shrugged slightly as much as to say: "What's the idea, we're from the same country, aren't we?" Like him, I wanted to talk about that remarkable story and I did not hesitate to engage in conversation him whom at once I took to be an accomplice.

"If, as they say," continued my new friend, "that Jane has confessed, they'll nab him pretty, because the damn fool must be in hiding."

"I don't think he's hiding."

"Then, they'll have a job to get their hands on him. That's a thing nobody wants to believe: as long as you keep moving, as long as you go on living, it's some job, take it from me, to track a person. It's a moving target. To know, and to be able to shut up and go on living, as if nothing had happened, as if you hadn't done a thing, there's the secret. It's a trick of the trade—take it from me, I'm wise to that all right."

"But what's your trade?"

"Thief. It's about the same thing, right? And you?"

"Nothing."

"Lucky guy. I don't know, though; listen, every trade has a good and a bad side. There's a thrill to being a thief. It's like the races. The only trouble is you have to win all the time."

I recognized the line and, because of the banality of word and thought, I lost no time in deciding that my questioner was a practical joker and listened to him carelessly. He rambled on like people who have held their tongues too long and who, once they have begun to talk, can't and don't know how to stop. While he was going on with his praise of a thief's life, I was examining him from head to foot being careful the while to appear quite unconcerned, an unnecessary precaution since he talked and talked without the least care in the world for what I might do or say. He was a young man of about thirty, big and strong, with piercing black eyes. The most prominent of his features were the two long ears standing out from the side of his head and the under lip which hung almost to the chin. A face, however, that had nothing monstrous about it; in looking at it you were impressed above all by the "cheek" of which it was the image. His slender, well-kept hands gesticulated nervously on the table. It was these which held the attention: quick, active and unconstrained hands.

On ending the conversation, I found myself doubting my doubts and I said to myself that, after all, it was quite possible and even probable that this man was really a thief. That prompt and spontaneous avowal which at first I had thought a joke might be perhaps no more than a sign of the audacity that I now read upon his face and in his hands.

"What'll you bet," said he to me, "that inside of two days, they'll get the sailor?"

"I guess you're right," I answered, "but are you sure it's the sailor who committed the crime?"

"Most likely. If *they* weren't sure, *they* wouldn't have let the papers in on it. Anyhow, I'll know all about it pretty soon. . . . We're having a meeting tonight," said he in a low voice after a moment's hesitation.

He had just finished the bottle of *vin gris* which he had ordered and I offered him a second round. I was greatly interested, and somewhat amazed, too, at the truly friendly bearing of one who confessed his profession with a sort of elegance.

"To what meeting do you refer?"

He then explained that on stated evenings several "friends" and he were in the habit of getting together to discuss certain affairs. One of these "friends", a thief also, was on the police force and acted as a kind of backhanded informer, so to speak. He would put it up to them at this meeting and, in all probability, the bogus police officer would be able to give a reply. He consulted his wrist watch and briskly holding out his hand, bade me farewell.

"You don't believe me, right?"

I understood vaguely that, regretting his confession, he sought to deceive me by raising a doubt in my mind.

I dived again into the reading of the papers, but with less interest, for it seemed to me the news was already stale.

However, my recollections, rendered more colorful by my conversation with the thief, still tormented me. I had to make a real effort to drive away from before my eyes the unsympathetic face of the sailor whom I had met in the corridor of the Gare d'Orsay. The details of the scene, which I called the scene of the betrayal, by reason of its very unreality were fast fading away. But that loiterer armed with his sack, that persistent sailor, continued to pursue me and I could not keep myself from calling him the assassin.

I dined hurriedly in a small bistro of the neighborhood and without zest started my nocturnal promenade. Leaving the quays, where the night wind was beginning its ravages, I entered the little garden of the Trocadéro at a slow walk, following the leisurely turns of its bicornate paths and stopping now and then to sit upon a bench. This hesitant wandering echoed the jerky pace of my thoughts. I was unable to fix the boundaries between imagination and memory. The little garden and its tiny mysteries grew dark without its being evident that the night had come. One was conscious of being in shadow but there was no soft nocturnal mist. Through the trees the Eiffel Tower took on an impassioned aspect and became a deed of bravery and of pride. She lost, surrounded by stars, her familiar and kindly air that the first years of the twentieth century had given her. At this hour, the garden was almost deserted. Voices alone indicated the presence of others. I dreamed. And she who, towering above me, defied I don't know what, drew me away from all those vain debates, those burdensome questionings. The Eiffel Tower became more living than I. I had known long since that looking at her from the foot rendered her metallic and architectural, that perceiving her from a distance made her symbolic, and that she changed her appearance and character depending upon whether one admired her from Pantin or Grenelle, from Montmartre, or the Point-du-Jour.

I amused myself, with memory as an aid, by indefinitely varying her silhouette as if I were examining her through a kaleidoscope. Mobility and grace of that sort rendered her sympathetic to me and made of her a veritable friend, living and almost gay. And that evening, to think of her as so near me gave me courage. I esteemed her because on looking at her I realized suddenly that she alone could wrestle with the night and would finally triumph since in the shadows of night and the blue wind of the sky, she seemed brighter than ever, more majestic.

I left her shadow and continued my walk. I headed for the place d'Jena leaving the Trocadéro behind me on my right, sad as a ruin.

In passing before the entrance to the aquarium, screened by a thicket, I heard a noise of rustling leaves. Someone was walking very near me on the forbidden lawns. I stopped, strained my ears and tried to see. I distinguished among the shadows a human form with stooped shoulders advancing slowly and stealthily.

Without moving, I watched the comings and goings of this individual. Noiselessly he vaulted the little gate that at night bars entrance to the aquarium, and passed within.

I believe I am one of the few inhabitants of Paris who know and haunt this artificial and despised grotto. Often in the morning I go to this cavern to admire the trout gliding among the plants and to marvel at the play of bubbles more beautiful than lace. The refreshing coolness of the place and above all the opalescent light seem to me even more to be admired than the silent and moonlike evolutions of the fish caught red-handed in the act of living. Through large glass panes one can watch the carp grow old, and see the play of the sun's beams.

This aquarium is a secret.

The noises I had heard now died away but my curiosity was aroused. What was the man doing at such an hour, in this obscure spot?

I hesitated but a moment before following. I climbed over the iron fence and as silently as possible I descended the first steps. A sound of voices, voices low by reason of the dark, came to me, but I could distinguish only a confused murmur. I could make out that there were several voices, three or perhaps four. Bravely I went down three more steps and advanced several paces, pressed close to the wall. I remembered a corner where the architect of the aquarium had constructed a settee. I intended to go there and sit down and, relying on the acoustics of the place, overhear the conversation.

At the entrance it was dark, but near the big carp pools the glimmer of a lamp lighted a few passages, forming great squares of luminous water where long fish floated half asleep. At the rear, in one of these squares of light, several heads were revealed, gaunt and pale, as it appeared to me. I was struck particularly by one of them for I recognized it without, however, being able to attach a name to it. Growing accustomed to that misty light, I was able, without fear of being discovered, to make out five men, busily engaged in a discussion and confident of being neither seen nor heard.

I could hardly listen for I was both astonished at this council and thrilled by the surroundings and this night wherein Paris was confiding to me another secret.

Thanks to the darkness and the weather, I was present at this council and only my memory seemed alert. The face of one of these persons held all my attention. I recognized it, and just as one struggles to identify a fleeting song, I puzzled over the name of the man whom my tenacious memory detached from the group. So suddenly that I was forced to check an exclamation at my very lips, I understood why it was impossible for me to remember his name. I didn't now it. He whom I had recognized was my interlocutor of the small café, the neighbor to whom I had offered a glass of wine.

It was the "meeting" of which he had spoken at which, involuntarily, and by what we wrongly call "chance", I was present. I listened from then on with all my ears, since undoubtedly it was a question of some nefarious scheme.

My curiosity was acute. Suddenly a name resounded in my ears because it was familiar to me: Georgette.

The obscurity from which jetted the flame of a girl's name rendered all thought void and encouraged reverie to the point of drunkenness. It seemed as though the right to follow the will-o'-the-wisp that flickered through this maze under the name of Georgette was not to be mine.

Everything whirled at the speed of my thought. I could not imagine that one night had followed another and that this woman nevertheless continued to impose her presence. Play of flames and plaything of the winds. Someone called for Georgette. She was there. The mention of her name, in fact, caused her to rise to her feet and, in the frame of one of the tanks I saw her, armed with her smile.

She described the scene at which, the night before, we had been silent witnesses. She spoke in a low voice but I knew the song, and it was easy for me to fill in the gaps in the story which she was relating.

I was expecting inventions, deviations, but her recital had the dryness and precision of a report. From time to time, she added a commentary, deprecations or approvals, which, however, gave no inkling of a final judgment on her own part.

The recital finished, she declared:

"Jules was there and another chap I didn't know."

"Suspicious?" asked someone.

"No," she replied disdainfully and Jules put in:

"Insignificant."

My ear had grown accustomed to the rise and fall of their voices and I followed easily the rest of their palaver.

"My guess," said one of them, "is they won't pick up the sailor yet a while, but they're sure going to find it necessary to do a little sweeping around here. We'd better be on our guard. As soon as we get through this business tonight, start working on your alibis. Right, Jules?"

"Yes, I'll be responsible for checking up on them," replied Jules who possessed a deep, bass voice.

"Let's clear out."

Noiselessly, Georgette departed. About five minutes elapsed. Now it was the turn of my table companion to quit the aquarium. One after another, after a short interval, the others abandoned the place. Being ignorant of their plans, I waited half an hour before going out; the avenue was deserted. A woman's umbrella lay flat on the sidewalk and a step or two beyond a glove had been forgotten on a bench. The Paris night grew big with shadows and these lost objects seemed to become a part of it.

CHAPTER THREE

I fled Him down the nights and down the days;
I fled Him, down the arches of the years;
I fled Him, down the labyrinthine ways
Of my own mind; and in the midst of tears
I hid from Him, and under running laughter.

—*Francis Thompson*

The days which followed that night were like a cloud. Motionless and mute, they left not a trace, not one regret. Paris was black and unconcerned. I think it rained softly, but soon after, a morose wind dried away all traces.

Paris swelled out with boredom, then slept as if to digest it. It was surely the moment to follow step by step in the wake of dreams.

And meanwhile, as if in answer to the city's signal, the small clock I used to measure time and ennui stopped each evening at eleven thirty-five. There was no explanation for this disconcerting regularity. One could accept this constancy as homage or as a habit. But by the fourth day, toward half past eleven, my heart was throbbing because I hoped that at last the patented time piece was about to lose this habit. At eleven thirty-five, before my eyes, the clock stopped with a significant click. Then my doorbell rang. A note for me, brought by a hotel messenger in a little cap, who in exchange for the letter asked for a tip. One of my friends wanted me to do him the great service of going to meet him in a hotel in the center of Paris. I am not one of those who deny the truth of miracles and when I question myself, I am ready to affirm that it is upon them alone that I can count. The cold, dull realm of actualities, arid and uncultivated as it is, has never tempted me as the goal for an expedition.

That providential letter was a hidden cry loosed by Paris, Paris who wanted me and who, once more, had chosen for this mission the name of a friend.

At the stand was a single taxi, which seemed to be impatiently awaiting my arrival. The chauffeur in opening the door for me had upon his face one of those "understanding" smiles which left little doubt in my mind. Full of zeal, he drove me to the hotel designated as swiftly as possible. I took pains to notice the time at each clock we passed on the trip, and on passing the seventeenth, I was astonished to observe that all, without exception, and despite the distance run, pointed to eleven thirty-five. Had time stopped? The intrepid chauffeur pushed his motor to the limit and seemed to comprehend the importance of his mission, an importance of which I was myself at that moment ignorant.

The taxi stopped before the hotel in the rue Saint-Honoré and sped off as soon as I stood upon the sidewalk and had paid the fee for the trip.

The little hotel is jammed between two houses and is unable to display more than one window per floor. It is gray, dirty, almost falling apart. A breeze always whistles about its door. Its shadow is a hole. Two silverware and jewelry shops close it in upon either side and cast the shapes of glowworms upon the sidewalk. I entered the hotel afraid I had made a mistake.

A huge woman, monstrous, came to meet me with a smile on her lips. She was abominably made up and so very amiable that she became a nonentity.

"Your friend Jacques is waiting for you," she told me. "Room 4, on the third."

The stairs were of a repellent filthiness. In the corners

were ranged household utensils and faded, dried-up flowers, which nevertheless were artfully displayed.

I opened the door of room 4 after having waited vainly for a response.

Jacques seemed to be weeping.

Jacques is a likeable boy, one who insists that he ranks trustworthiness and kindness above all the other virtues. But he is prodigiously and furiously selfish, profits thereby and prides himself upon it. Of course I had never before seen him weep and I noticed that he was a poor hand indeed at shedding tears.

"My dear fellow," said he.

Jacques started his lamentations, then apologized; I understood finally that he was in love, and in the worst way—without reason, without pleasure, with a disconcerting obstinacy.

Jacques is an egotist but he is also headstrong.

He began by telling me of his walks about Paris and of the delights they afforded him, coming at last to the happening which he described extraordinary.

One night, around two, he was seated before a café looking at the passers-by and sizing up the women. As a challenge to himself, he thought to speak to a prostitute who was approaching with the rather overconspicuous dignity of a young woman coming out of the theater. He followed her, intending to speak to her, but in vain, for she quickened her pace the moment she felt that Jacques was gaining ground.

She led him to the banks of the Seine, and instead of following the quays, she slipped into the icy shadow of the Louvre, and skirted the railing which now replaces the moat.

Thus they arrived before the church of Saint-Germain-l'Auxerrois. The young woman paused a few seconds to adjust some part of her dress and Jacques took the opportunity to ask her where she was going, but she did not answer. She resumed her way and plunged into the rue des Prêtres-Saint-Germain-l'Auxerrois. Jacques was at her side and now could see her face, close up, lit suddenly by the light of a street lamp. He found her pale and charming and this discovery determined him to show more eagerness. He seized her arm, asking permission, most unnecessarily, to accompany her. But with a brusque and energetic movement, she escaped his grasp, took a few steps at a run. Then Jacques suffered an instant of discouragement. He turned his back, but suddenly regretting his momentary decision, sought again to take up the pursuit. He saw no one. Annoyed by this disappearance which thwarted his plans, he searched anxiously for the young woman. His pains were lost. He waited, not daring to quit this sinister little street where, nevertheless, he hoped to see that charming face again. An hour passed. He heard a scream, then a kind of murmur. Jacques, being an egotist, felt little curiosity. He left the rue des Prêtres-Saint-Germain-l'Auxerrois without hastening to the place whence the cry had come. Discouraged and most dissatisfied, he hailed a taxi and had himself driven home.

But in spite of the chase, despite the vigil and the disappointment, Jacques confessed to me that he could not sleep and that for the whole night he could think of nothing but the empty hours that hummed past in painful silence.

He sought my advice. Two days and two nights without sleep, two nights during which he had wrestled, now with forgetfulness and now with the memory of a pale face. Finally, the day before, exhausted, beside himself, he had followed several women, slept with three of them, drunk, tramped the streets, and dawn had found him in this hotel room beside a middle-aged female who, in unexpurgated language, was proposing obscene and vicious practices. Incapable of leaving the room or even getting up, stupefied but wide awake, he had mentally retraced his steps about

Paris, followed his comings and goings in memory, desperate and ready for anything.

I was not slow in urging him to find the woman, and even volunteered to aid him in his search.

Quickly we paid for the room and losing not an instant, we betook ourselves to the scene of the meeting, persuaded as I was that the pale young woman, this night as on all others, would follow her customary path.

With red liqueurs before us, we awaited the appointed hour, watching faces and discussing the prospects for the night.

As the night advanced, to pass the time we discussed the changes in the little street. Every quarter of an hour saw a flood and an ebb. Then uneasiness took possession of us. The hour when Jacques had met his love was approaching. And at this moment it was no longer a woman for whom we were lying in wait, but a certainty which we craved, filled with the anxiety one experiences while waiting for a roulette ball to stop on a certain number. In the fluctuating light we were aware of this uncertainty; in the vacillations of the street we discovered that long minute which precedes a certitude.

By common accord we had grown silent, the eyes of both

fixed upon the corner of the street *where she was to appear.*

Just when the silence had become really intolerable I felt an imperative need (I do not exaggerate) to tell Jacques the strange drama which I had witnessed, and everything that had followed it—the wanderings, the strange sights and encounters. Unconsciously I made Paris play the lead.

Despite his apparent anguish—much like that of an actor or a gambler—Jacques breathed hard and cut in with: "And then? . . ." I hesitated to tell him the whole truth, surprised myself to hear this recital in which chance gave to my comings and goings and to all my adventures the glamour of miracles.

And just as I spoke the name of Georgette, Jacques gave me an evil look.

"Shut up," said he, "there she is."

And quite so, I saw a pale young woman emerge from the shadows, walking with slow, short steps.

Our decision was quickly made: at a distance of a few yards we walked behind her, behind Georgette whom Jacques thought he loved, whom I myself had recognized.

Passing before the Institute, Jacques squeezed my arm, inclined to be afraid. The darkness was so thick that at every step we thought to stumble. Jacques, more than I perhaps, kept thinking about my story. He sought traces of it and the sinister scene corresponded with my descriptions.

Calmer now, I was able to recognize the landscape which I saw as just one more of the aspects of Paris. Yet on approaching the quays where the shadow of Georgette was cast in profile, I was astonished to find myself in this place which seemed to me even more tragic than my imagination had pictured it since the grand scene. I realized the surprising force of substitutions. I was wrong in believing that I had remembered the noise of the wind, the faint light of the street lamps, the voluptuous murmur of the river. Dates grew confused. Time was lost in the enormous shadows and destroyed by the presence of this woman.

I felt like calling to Georgette and, but for the presence of Jacques, I think I should have shouted out, to dissipate the mirage of recollection and actuality, to separate past from present, to break time into bits. But he refused to turn from that shadow which continued on its way. Jacques was certainly more eager to know where she was going than to take her by the arm or to kiss her lips. I realized that he was plainly more in love with the mystery than with the woman who was proceeding according to her destiny.

She was picked up, near the Pont-Neuf, by some sort of student in a béret who was taken by her to a hotel room. With decision, Jacques bribed the patron of the hotel and obtained the room next to that in which the student was undressing. We were misled by the banality of that interview. Georgette first demanded her pay, then, having complained about its smallness, declared that she was in a hurry because of a rendezvous with a Spaniard.

Jacques and I made no secret of our joy. Georgette was no more than an ordinary prostitute; and by ourselves we had manufactured a mystery out of whole cloth. But now we were inclined to abandon our pursuit or, to do the thing up properly, to lie with Georgette.

However, when the characteristic noises and the succeeding silence indicated to us that all was over, we quitted the room and took up our watch at the door of the hotel. We wanted at least to make the acquaintance of the Spaniard.

Georgette resumed her stroll about Paris, through the mazes of the night. She went on, dispelling sorrow, solitude or tribulation. Then more than ever did she display her strange power: that of transfiguring the night. Thanks to her, who was no more than one of the hundred thousands, the Parisian night became a mysterious domain, a great and marvelous country, full of flowers, of birds, of glances and of stars, a hope launched into space. . . . Slave of my impressions, I thought of a velodrome.

Jacques promptly called to my attention that Georgette, contrary to what she had stated, seemed in no haste and furthermore that she was following exactly the same path as when he had met her the first time. Jacques for his part was obsessed with thoughts of a gigantic clock.

That night, as we were pursuing or, more exactly, tracking Georgette, I saw Paris for the first time. It was surely not the same city. It lifted itself above the mists, rotating like the earth on its axis, more feminine than usual. As I looked at it, it contracted. And Georgette herself became a city.

When we had arrived before the Palais Royal, Jacques gave me to understand that he preferred to be alone. He thanked me and promised to tell me the further course and outcome of his adventure.

I left him then but in no haste and without regret. The avenue de l'Opéra was no longer the stream that I had always followed, nor the highway that one usually pictures. It was a great shadow flashing like a glacier, which one must first conquer, and then embrace as one would a woman.

In the distance floated the Iceberg, the huge mass of the

Opéra which trembled under the weight of approaching morning. From one minute to the next I expected that it would capsize at one stroke, thus signaling the waiting belfries to toll the angelus.

Next day, and the days following, I waited in vain for news from Jacques. I called him up.

He replied that he had slept with Georgette.

"And then?" said I.

"Nothing much," replied he. And spoke of other matters.

But at this moment a storm arose to the east of Paris.

CHAPTER FOUR

I was, of course, determined not to lose track of this singular young woman who seemed to follow a career still more strange than her shadow. I hoped surely to run across her one night or another and not to leave her until I had discovered her true identity.

More than anything else I called to mind her face, still childish but already betraying signs of age. Her gestures described peculiar zigzags, disquieting and seductive at the same time. She seemed to be surrounded by an exhalation of uncertain hue.

I realized perfectly that in appearance she was just a common prostitute, the sister of all the prostitutes who overrun Paris and who, they say, are all more or less alike. But Georgette was seductive only because she was somehow different and because her appearance was obviously deceptive.

Behind the everyday veil, under her make-up, one could discern her real flesh and could, so to speak, breathe her proper perfume, her very essence.

But what gave her person a charm that could be described as special was her resemblance to a shadow. One might well be astonished, and I never failed to be so, by her strange ability to escape judgment. She resembled at times gleams of light, at times their sisters the shadows. Before memory and words she was evasive as a fish. She withdrew, even while she remained present, or even when she became burdensome and immense.

I could not better picture her to myself than by the words: the smile of a shadow.

This resemblance became more pronounced when one thought of her manner of living. She loved only the dark which she seemed each night to wed and her charm itself did not become real until she withdrew from the light to enter obscurity. Looking closely at her one could not picture her as living during the day. She was the night itself and her beauty was nocturnal.

Just as one says quite unconsciously: clear as day, so one could not avoid finding Georgette beautiful as night. I think of her eyes, of her teeth, her hands, of that pallor which covered her entire body. And I do not forget that refreshing coolness which was part of it all.

It seemed to me that Georgette grew more desirable as the night advanced, that each hour divested her of a garment and gradually revealed her nudity.

All these are but memories that delude and inflame, all are desires of the night, but Georgette had understood that, to be beautiful and desired, she must identify herself with the night, with the quotidian mystery.

I sought her and this pursuit brought her closer to me. Chance surprises overmuch. I sought her and soon I was able to find her.

With astonishing persistence, she was patrolling the block between the rue de Seine and the rue de Buci. There was no suggestion of melancholy about her. At times she would stop before a café and look the customers over, shrugging her shoulders when she perceived some among them playing cards. Toward eleven, when the cafés closed, she left these streets and headed for the Seine. Whenever a man spoke to her, she examined him rapidly and more often than not begged him to be on his way. Once in a while she'd take his arm and accompany him to a dark little hotel. Then a few moments after she would proceed with her walk. Often, furtive women, trembling either from cold or desire, I do not know which, would accost her and I was astonished never to see her refuse their offers. There was such a regularity in her habits that I was the first to laugh at them.

Several nights I was able to observe her without arousing her suspicion of this surveillance. One night, though, she recognized me, in passing. She came toward me and inquired, "How are you?" Then she continued her walk. I followed her when she left the rue de Seine. She made for the quays and rapidly crossed the Pont-Neuf. Arrived before Saint-Germain-l'Auxerrois, she quickened her pace and entered the small rue des Prêtres-Saint-Germain-l'Auxerrois. She seemed to have disappeared in the darkness. Soon I saw her again near the railings of the Louvre. She knew her way so well that she seemed to follow it with closed eyes. I could see her lowered eyelids. That night she did not seem to be aware of my presence a few yards behind her. The wind whistled past me and then went to sing around the great gates of the Louvre. A passer-by dragged his cane against the railings, the strollers' imbecilic xylophone. The deep shadows of the great building formed a background against which the stars revolved as on a dial.

Georgette walked at a slow pace, like one with time at her disposal who makes the most of it. But instead of interrupting her walk by stops before half-open shop windows, she paused to contemplate the sky or now and again to look at herself in a mirror. She feared neither cold, nor rain, nor the malediction of the wind.

Under the arcades of the rue de Rivoli, she amused herself by looking at her hands or, more often still, by humming a little song of which certain snatches reached my ears, but very little, for she sang for herself alone.

Of course, men stopped to speak to her and she listened with courtesy, replying to them graciously, now accepting their proposals, now rejecting them. In each little street she knew some gloomy small hotel.

Georgette never seemed to hesitate. Arrived before the Palais Royal, she drew her cloak about her, knowing the metallic cold that oozes from the walls. Then she pulled her hat down slightly and with a determined step passed beneath the galleries. Women with bent backs and haggard eyes were walking slowly about. Their walk never let up, their eyes remained fixed on the ground, their hands hidden under their coats. Each time that Georgette crossed before one of these creatures, she said, "Good evening" and the salutation sounded like a laugh.

For a few minutes a slight fear grips him who ventures into this rectangle. Suddenly one senses the presence of music floating about like smoke. One cannot say, to be sure, that he perceives it, but it moves about and makes itself felt. It creeps along the deserted paths, clings to the branches of the shrubbery, overwhelms the statues. It is a music that one sees but no longer hears since at this hour it is but the memory of music. Often a glimmer of light outlines a window atop a wing of the Palais and one knows that he is in a prison because the night becomes so threatening.

Georgette alone was not subject to this power which invaded the garden and licked at the long blank buildings like flames. Georgette passed quietly through the obstacles raised by these night hours, obstacles that almost seemed to be the corpses of those hours.

A somber fellow was striding about the four galleries looking neither to right nor left. He was following one dream and struggling with another dream. Georgette stopped to touch him. But he did not turn his head.

It was in the Palais Royal that I saw Georgette at her trade. Her care and the attention she gave to every detail left not a doubt. When chance or habit sent a man her way, she leaned toward the victim and showed him her hands. Observed somewhat from a distance, this proceeding was a miracle. She drew him gently but irresistibly toward one of the corners which the darkness transforms into a bottomless pit. And there . . .

She returned quickly into the half-light and shook herself like a bird. With the same sharp movement, she pulled down her hat a little, then wrapped herself in her cloak and, walking the while, kept upon the watch.

The night advanced. The little light high up went out and Georgette took up her march. Once more she made the turn of the garden but her gait made it plain that it was the last.

Still bird-like, she slipped away from the Palais Royal and, walking faster, went along the rue Saint-Honoré yet filled with dusk. The hour seemed to disquiet Georgette for she walked faster and faster. She had become an ordinary woman in a hurry, going early to work, a chilly woman just out of bed. No doubt she already felt the day. She stopped several minutes, however, before the hotel where Jacques had asked me to meet him. It was more drab and sinister than ever, a roost for birds of misfortune.

She called softly, as do certain owls, her own name: "Georgette"—and soon the door of the hotel opened. A woman, what looked like a woman, stuck out her head. She was thin and ugly, with the ugliness of early morning. Georgette went in for a few moments then, more bold than ever, reappeared to head toward the Champs-Elysées.

I knew very well now that she was bound for her post near the Petit Palais where I had found her again at the close of that night which for me was memorable. It was now more evident to me than it had been on the first occasion that Georgette was on her way to prowl about this architectural skeleton—ready to satisfy the strange desires of those who walk in the Champs-Elysées at dawn.

Georgette was plainly aware of the hour, for she kept looking at the shamefaced strollers who were hiding behind the trees or who, with assumed indifference, were enjoying a cigarette and the end of the night.

But on that particular night my mind was made up not to be surprised by the birth of day and to follow Georgette, in spite of the cold and the daylight.

Several times she leaned toward beings who looked desolate. Some among them seemed habitués, so evident were the precision and the rapidity of their gestures.

Day had come. Now the glimmer sprang and caught among the trees, now it rose like a tide, imperceptibly submerging the greenswards and the horizon. Soon I was able to distinguish women near the Petit Palais. They grew bigger with the day and moved more slowly. It almost seemed that something had announced the passing of the hour. The Champs-Elysées looked completely deserted.

Suddenly a taxi burst from the place de la Concorde, going at top speed, as if frightened by the silence of this jungle.

In the midst of a small group, Georgette made her way toward the subway, the gates of which were just being opened. Their hands full of confessions, of shames, of sighs, the prostitutes of the Champs-Elysées plunged into the mouth of the metro as gaily as a crowd of midinettes leaving the work rooms. They were laughing, talking about fair weather and rain, ribbons and lingerie, shoes and hats. I even had the impression that if a millionaire lost in the metro were now to offer them a fortune to abstain from certain vulgar amorous practices, they would all have refused.

Collar turned up, unshaven, I was watching Georgette whose laughter was as frequent as any. She rummaged in her bag for dress samples which she offered for approval. The precautions I took to make myself unrecognizable were quite useless for she would not have known me. She no longer had her nocturnal eyes.

I was determined, as a sick man can be, to find out and know her complete existence, to follow her tracks through the day and through sleep.

Toward five in the morning one is possessed of a clarity that is almost perfect for it derives not from the body but emanates solely from the brain.

At the Châtelet Station, Georgette alighted and turned toward the Cité. Slowly I followed her through one of the long passages which lead to an exit. The crowd was not so dense as in the evening but already there were a good number using the subway. Lovers have used this celebrated passageway as a meeting place since the opening of the line. At all hours of the day dozens of couples can be seen here, pressed close together, offering their lips and their hands, without thinking of appearances. Neither the occasional passer-by nor sharp drafts can disturb these embraces. Each couple seems to believe itself invisible.

Georgette, accustomed to these amorous scenes, picked her way past these groups of wan but avid lovers, who at this hour were still half-asleep in the midst of their passion.

The day was breaking. Georgette said good-bye to one of her companions and quickened her steps.

I had never seen her in full daylight and I shrank from the revelation. I suspected that the mystery which enveloped her would suddenly evaporate.

Then I saw her, but she was no longer the same. Here was an uninspired woman, commonplace and hardy. Probably she no longer knew how to smile. She was lost in the crowd, a part of it. Never could I have picked her out.

She went to the baker's, to the milkman and each said to her: "Good morning, Miss." Now and again she shook hands with one of the shopkeepers. All the evidences of respectability. . . . But when I thought of what she had been, which some would have loved to call queen of mystery, I would rather have seen her dead at my feet.

She was everything that one would expect in a twenty-two-year-old girl.

She stopped before a house in the narrowest part of the rue de Seine, not far from the quays. At the rear of the court she climbed a narrow stairway to the fifth floor.

Day splashed the casing of the stairs; and all the blemishes wrought by time appeared. Georgette opened a door.

CHAPTER FIVE

*O, Treïul, remember that we are of the same race
and that I am entitled to your aid.*

—*Raymond Roussel* (LA POUSSIÈRE DE SOLEIL)

Days succeeded nights. The mystery which surrounded
Georgette had not been dispersed but it appeared less dense
to me.

Time was digging a pit.

Nevertheless, a sort of aimless impatience would occa-
sionally take hold of me as some scene presented itself to
my eyes. At such times I was again lost in those shadows
where the traces or the presence of Georgette seemed in-
dispensable. But as soon as day came my impatience was
destroyed and only in a vague way did I think of executing
my project. For several nights I had thought of going to the

rue de Seine, of climbing the stairs once more and knocking at that small door which she had opened. But it was night that summoned Georgette, and day drove her from my memory just as it drove her from the streets of Paris.

Not only chance was responsible for this, but also those gaps in time which result in a kind of abstraction that in turn fosters an inability to overcome the least obstacle. The day came when I resolved, much as if I were gambling, that cost what it might I would find Georgette again—her whom I called Georgette of the night. It was winter and five in the afternoon. I jumped into a taxi to end my hesitation and presented myself at the rue de Seine. I had, of course, prepared a little speech to excuse my indiscretion and my curiosity. I knocked at the door and a man opened it to me. I was not expecting to find myself in the presence of a big chap like that and thought I had mistaken the door. I was silent for a while before I could mumble a few words of excuse. Then, however, I heard the voice of a woman ask:

"Who is it, Octave?"

By a turn of his chin, Octave passed the question on to me and I had to answer as quickly as possible.

"Pardon me for disturbing you but I wish to speak to Mademoiselle Georgette."

"This is the place," replied Octave. There was nothing in his tone that appeared menacing to me but I was nevertheless greatly surprised when he stepped back to let me enter. My mind had rapidly jumped to the obvious conclusion, that Octave was a pimp. Looking at him nearer, while he was closing the door, I saw clearly that there was nothing of the bully about him. Octave certainly did not appear to be one of those who have been dubbed with that fine title, professional vagabonds.

By the light of an oil lamp, before a table covered with what seemed an immaculate oilcloth, Georgette was sewing. Near her workbasket lay a drawing board, paints, a small goblet of water and a few brushes.

"You have come for some drawings, sir?" asked Georgette, and I couldn't tell whether she spoke in this way to deceive me or to deceive Octave. I was careful not to contradict and passed myself off as an art lover.

Sweetly, oh so sweetly, Georgette, still sitting in the lamp light, reeled off one stupidly flattering remark after another in praise of Octave's no less stupid work, which rested on her knees. The whole scene was oh so commonplace and proper. But all at once she asked a question: "Don't you think my brother makes pretty drawings?" So Octave was her brother, I could not help but say, with a shade of astonishment in my voice.

"Indeed he *is*, sir."

And she resumed her explanations. On the walls were pinned watercolor sketches, flowers, feathers, birds, landscapes where glided a boat, always the same boat. "My brother knows how to draw and can do whatever is wanted. He paints trees, lakes, mountains." On the other side of the chinks in the shutters, day had come to a close. One could still make out patches of light in the sky. Georgette was still the servant of the day. Her vacant eyes were puffy, her mouth was shapeless and her lips pale. Her hands trotted about like domestic animals and her voice was white and cold.

I asked questions. She replied with the greatest willingness imaginable while Octave, immobile, more and more abstracted, seemed to be playing with a shadow.

Octave, Georgette told me, was a serious student. He was attending evening classes and showed a decided taste for painting; he devoted all his spare time to it. Incapable of the least falsehood, he had been the pride of his parents when both died within a few weeks of each other. Before their death, Octave had been "in retreat" and associated with no

63

companions. Everyone sang his praises; he loved precision and sought always to go to the bottom of things. They said of him in the quarter: "He's a fine fellow."

Octave was not listening and Georgette spoke as if in the presence of a deaf person. While tracing the portrait of the young Octave, she seemed to be weaving the tapestry of their common youth. She kept tossing her head.

Meanwhile night was falling and the darkness penetrated into the room, closing about the lamp. A smell of stew came up the stairs. Little by little noises were muted, one by one, while Georgette went on talking more softly. Her voice was a song. "We had to live," she was saying. "I suggested to Octave that I go to work. He was so tired. No one wanted him. I know Paris; and we are placed on this earth to live. Everything is so simple when one knows all the streets as I do, and all the people who move in them. They are all seeking something without seeming to do so." Night came closer and closer, more and more tangible, and Georgette herself was drawing nearer to me. Octave was staring at his finger nails fixedly. He was hiding himself behind darkness and immobility. As I questioned Georgette, I saw him raise his eyes to the clock, look at it a long time, then take out his watch and compare it with the clock.

He frowned, placed his watch on the table, and, his head between his hands, lost himself in contemplation of its face.

While watching these maneuvers of Octave, these tacit pleas for his habitual silence, I noticed the happiness of Georgette who now was talking as if she were unable to stop. But the more night deepened, the more her words were divorced from her subject. She had talked at first of her brother, then gradually she abandoned him to chant the praises of Paris. Before my eyes I saw her change. Her lips grew red, color came into her cheeks, her eyes shone with a singular brightness. Little by little I saw that at last she recognized me. She laid down her work and listened to the striking of the hour from a nearby steeple.

After the manner of those who sing in the music halls, almost in the same words, she told of her affection and tenderness for Paris. One could almost see a sparrow flying and hear a pastry cook or a little messenger boy whistling the latest song. Looking at Georgette I was reminded of that diminutive woman near the porte d'Orléans, who used to sing the latest song hits to the accompaniment of an accordion and a guitar. The musicians were always surrounded by a large circle of admirers and pupils, who tried to memorize the air of the song which had just been sold them for ten cents, one dime. The young songstress shouted her song to the skies, singing for the trees which towered above the crowd. In listening to it I seemed to hear only an echo. The atmosphere of the room became unbearable; the presence of the silent Octave and the metamorphosis of this woman, whom the street was already calling almost against her will, made the monotonous tacking about of the minutes all too apparent. A certain constraint colored these transformations, these appeals and these silences.

I left the room hurriedly, promising to come again soon in order to cover my retreat. I promised it in good faith and in actuality kept my promise for, two days later, around ten in the evening, I pushed the door half-open.

Georgette had just gone out. The bittersweet scent with which she wraps herself as in a scarf still lingered in the room. Octave was looking at the clock with great attention. I might have thought that, since my first visit, he had changed neither his position nor even his occupation.

I was able to observe him at my ease without his deigning to take notice of my presence. He was a big chap of about twenty, thin, bony, with great arms and long legs. His hands rather than his face held the attention. They were dead hands:

pale, long and rigid like hands of plaster. His face was set, neither sad nor gay, and when he smiled he remained perfectly indifferent. The sole evidence of character were signs of stubbornness which were also signs of will power. In looking at his eyes, his lips, his chin, one saw that Octave finished whatever he started.

That night I was able to talk a long time with Octave, who unbent little by little. The later the hour, the more loquacious he became. Toward two in the morning I even found that he took great pleasure in narrating.

Octave has all sorts of hobbies. What he loves above all else is to try experiments. He has to experiment with everything to see what happens. Thus in the morning when Georgette returns he puts his milk and coffee in his soup to know what this mixture will taste like. Some time ago he went out one evening and went to "Montmartre" to sleep with a woman. It was, he assured me, the first time. It did not impress him at all. She suggested certain special practices to him. At first he had a feeling of repugnance, but soon he told himself that he must see what it was like. This very morning he had stretched himself on his bed to know the sensation of smoking lying down. He stood for an hour "to see what that was like."

He stopped talking suddenly and began to count the number of hairs in a paint brush.

Then, in spite of my questions, he relapsed into silence like someone drowning.

Wasted effort. Octave had departed, and for a realm to which I could not follow him. He seemed to push aside the horizon, drive back the walls of the room, wipe out the boundaries of day and dismiss the objects which surrounded us. At first believing him tired after his long confession, I turned my back on him and partly opened the window and the shutters to glance out over the surrounding territory.

There were the usual corrugated tin roofs and forests of chimneys, above which appeared steeples, cupolas, and a taller chimney more imposing than the others. What struck me most was that instead of the expected darkness I saw a red sky, the red not of blood but of flames. The city seemed to be surrounded by a flaming aureole, an aurora borealis, red and mysterious.

Noises mingled with this strange almost liquid red. Certain of them, however, detached themselves sharply from the confused humming and seemed to burst like a bubble.

Heard from afar it became one great sound, rising like a column. Then, as if by chance, a window quite close to the one in which I was now leaning, resting on my elbows, sprang to life. It seemed immense. A man had just lit an oil lamp in a neighboring room. He thought himself alone, not aware that anyone could see him. He removed his coat and jacket. His hat on his head, now in shirt sleeves, he opened a large wallet and began to count bank notes.

From time to time, as if in play, he applauded silently, and then went to take a swallow from a glass standing on the chimney piece. When he had finished his little calculations, he bent over a newspaper which he had unfolded and crisscrossed it with pencil marks.

Octave, himself again, had joined me and, seeing the man, smiled for the first time that evening.

"He's a bookie—"

". . . . . ?"

"He's a friend," he finished.

He gave a long whistle and the man came to the window, opened it, and cried:

"Hello, Octave. Are you coming Sunday to Vincennes?"

Octave raised his arms to signify his uncertainty. Then he closed the shutters, the window, put on his cap, blew out the lamp, and we descended the stairs—very slowly, for often Octave would stop before a door and seem to ponder deeply. He continued the descent but more and more heavily and reluctantly. I almost thought that the street frightened him, or that he dreaded the emptiness of night or the lonely flight of the hours that follow midnight. But it was doubtless some other fear, for Octave, who now seemed to be taking his courage in both hands, was more and more clearly flying from some inner spectacle. He was loath to leave the little fifth story room.

In the deserted street he plunged forward, closing his eyes. I was aware of nothing but the cold and the uneasiness inspired by this desperate, stolid creature with an evil mouth, more silent than the silence of the streets. Presently he entered a small café, the only one in the neighborhood that was still open, which seemed to struggle against the evil charm imposed by the hour. Two customers were talking together rather than drinking. One of them, in a faded soft felt hat, was he who had been counting his bills in the little room and had shouted to Octave. It was the same man that I had met under the vaulting of the Institute passageway, who had talked in a low voice. I recognized first of all his face, worn out like his clothes, his surprising blond moustache, his flat nose, his expressionless blue eyes. He shook Octave's hand but without putting any friendship into the gesture, emphasizing it so brutally that it became a gesture of domination, a mark of possession. And, for a fact, Octave obeyed him thenceforth, watching his hand and eye. His look never quitted him, seeming to await an order or a dismissal. The fourth of our party, whom I did not know or did not recognize, was a little bearded chap who merited being taken for a jolly good fellow. He was always laughing in his beard and wrinkling his eyes. It was plain that our two new companions distrusted me and sought unsuccessfully to explain my presence.

Suddenly we were united by one who was not present. I don't recall who amongst us pronounced the name of Georgette. But the fact is that the ice was immediately broken.

"Georgette," said the man in the felt hat, "owes us her silence. She has nothing to tell. She is out of all this."

"Don't agree with you, old man," replied the beard. "She has her word to say."

Octave shook his head but seemed to wish not to take part in the discussion.

"One of two things," took up the man in the soft hat. "Either she is with us, or she's against us. I was close beside her when this whole affair of Volpe's took place. She never peeped, nor I either, for that matter. We let the thing go on and she's got to stick it out. What's the idea of going and telling what you know? Volpe has the right to do what he pleases. He is stronger than us. . . ."

The man laid down these words before us like so many playing cards. Sharply and unexpectedly they revived the unexplained and unexplainable scenes which I had witnessed. Once more chance had destroyed oblivion, and given reality to what I would willingly think of as dreams. The words spoken by the friend and neighbor of Octave came and went, painting a picture over again, lighting all that space which my will and common sense had declared empty.

I was thrust back upon a faded memory which, with the power of a rebound, assumed all its clarity. This memory brought mystery in its train.

A sort of fury gripped me. I burned with a desire to demand explanations, to cry out that I understood nothing, but the little bearded chap got up and, before I could anticipate his gesture, seized a carafe from a neighboring table and smashed it on the marble table around which we were seated. We were all splashed but I alone paid heed.

"Always the same," said the man in the hat. Octave twisted his lips in disgust.

At that moment the action of the beard seemed natural to me. But it had the immediate effect of destroying my fury.

"Yes, always the same," cried the man in the beard. "Georgette has the right to do what she pleases. I understand nothing of this affair of Volpe's. What's the meaning of all this stage setting? Is he, yes or no, a cop? Is he an amateur? The woman has confessed because they forced her to confess. And then? Georgette is right to have her doubts, I also have my doubts and you, too, into the bargain."

"No."

"Positively. The proof is that you haven't dared speak to Georgette. You want it to be Octave who keeps her from saying what she thinks."

It made one feel like laughing to look at him who was expected to wrestle with the absentee. He was quite lost in contemplation of a slot machine, suspended here in the midst of all these ideas that assailed him from every side. He may have been in search of some sort of perpetual motion.

Very clearly I was the only one still listening to the discussion of the two comrades, and I was divided between the desire to question and that of keeping my mouth shut in order to learn more.

At this moment the proprietor of the café summoned the man in the slouch hat under pretext that he was wanted on the telephone.

"What an affair!" said I, addressing myself to the little chap in the beard, hoping for a response.

"There is no affair," said he with a smile.

"Vincennes," said Octave simply to the man in the hat, who was now returning. Then he got up and I followed him.

His hands in his pockets like a sailor, Octave headed for the quays and toward Notre-Dame. We walked along the branch of the Seine which encircles the Île de la Cité, where the water sleeps in the shadow of the dead Cathedral.

He descended to the river bank and without saying a word sat at the foot of the wall. Several sleepers lay near us sheltered from the wind.

The water slept. Octave watched. On the heels of this silence came the dawn, which made me flee far from his side, still overcome with amazement at all these sayings and doings. My ears were ringing.

CHAPTER SIX

I dreaded the monotony of the unknown. The domain through which I had just been passing where Georgette and Octave performed their evolutions now seemed a garden with well-worn paths. I wished to know nothing more of that mystery, which I accepted once and for all along with so many others. We do not have a taste for nor pleasure in mysteries save when we meet them head on.

I was ready to forget everything relating to those days, to relegate into oblivion those nights spent in the light of a woman's eyes. My mind made up, I decided that the surest way to dissipate this annoying fog and to answer the questions I put to myself about all these comings and goings was to become one of the crowd and to look upon Georgette as the most commonplace of prostitutes—that is to say, to spend an hour with her in the seclusion of a small hotel room.

One night I stationed myself to await the expected passing of her whom I now thought of as Octave's sister.

I had not waited long when I saw Georgette, coming along at her bird-like gait, pale and resolute—as resolute as I myself. I accosted her in the usual fashion, near the Louvre. She made as if she did not recognize me and led me at once to a house of assignation. Everything seemed ready to receive us and I admired the tact of the service. Of course they demanded a deposit which I gladly gave, more amused than aroused. I was, however, impatient enough to watch Georgette in the exercise of her profession and to see her nude.

As soon as we were alone in that frightfully shabby mauve room, it was impossible for me to keep from recalling Octave. That irresistible remembrance arose from Georgette's look, at this moment a perfect counterpart of her brother's. She seemed to be sleeping with open eyes. The precision of her queries and of her gestures at the moment of undressing made me doubt her existence. She folded her garments and placed them on the chair with the disconcerting rapidity of a juggler.

In all the exchanges which followed, she showed the same detached virtuosity.

Then she went on her way and left me at once astonished and reassured. I had almost the desire to applaud.

Reentering the cold streets I understood that the trap I had set for this woman had been most naïve. All too easy had it been for her to escape it. While I was clasping her in my arms, when I held my lips pressed against hers and bent my look to her eyes, she was living elsewhere, perhaps in another room, and only her shadow responded to my questions and my appeals.

I was not in despair but I realized with regret that the experiment attempted under such conditions had been useless. Impossible, assuredly, to drive off this shadow or to destroy it.

Afterwards, that evening, I resigned myself to expecting nothing of chance. I preferred certainty. But once again I was wrong to hold in small account decisions of which I was ignorant. I was following the rue Saint-Honoré in search of a tobacco shop which would still be open at this hour when, from around the corner of the rue de l'Échelle burst Octave, who appeared simply gigantic to me. He did not see me but continued on his way. I hesitated a moment to follow him, but curiosity was too strong and as silently as possible I fell into his pace. He, too, in his turn, seemed to be trying an experiment but he was more systematic than I.

His steps sounded with perfect regularity, as though this nocturnal prowler were counting them in a low voice. When he had come to the Opéra he stopped and seated himself on the steps of the National Academy of Music and the Dance. He had his eyes closed and at his feet, like a good dog, lay his cap. He seemed tired and heavy with sleep, but his attitude told me that this halt was to be brief. From the sleeping Opéra were borne great gusts of wind which surrounded him without his deigning to give heed. The lamps which are so numerous in this place cast a dirty, dull light, which made one cold. Occasionally passers-by crossed the square without even looking at Octave, immobile near the group of the Danse. Complete indifference everywhere. Octave belonged to the night. At last he got up and began again his regular walk. He did not stop until he reached the Pont de l'Europe, where he turned his back on the Gare Saint-Lazare to look down into the railroad cut, which made a gap among the buildings, and at the befouled advertisements more lugubrious still than the surrounding walls. One of them was torn and hung like a great dead hand above the shining tracks of the railroad. Here and there the red point of an electric lamp, as sad as the dead body of a dog. The cars on the switches looked like pretentious tombs.

Octave took up his walk. It was like the refrain of a hackneyed ditty, haunting and melancholy. He followed the path of the railway, as if he feared to leave the bright rails. Little by little we left Paris behind. Already the districts we were traversing had lost their Parisian color, just as the polar regions are shown faded out on geographic maps. We went past tall gray dwellings armed with windows, anonymous and mute. The streets crossed each other joylessly, like paths in a sunless forest. We came out at place Pereire where a taxi was making a turn, honking itself to death. One thought of an ant hill. At the center of the square, facing the small local station, a newspaper was playing with itself, blown here and there, on the loose.

Soon we passed the gates of Paris to enter the factory

district. The streets were bordered by long, bare and dirty walls, and night grew ever more black. Some posters burst out all at once at the corner of a boulevard. In the distance sang the lights of a café.

Carried away by our walk we lost track of passing time and the way grew so monotonous that we forgot the hours we had put behind us.

We left Levallois-Perret, extension of Paris, and approached the suburbs, which, I recall, appeared before us after crossing a something or other rue Émile-Zola.

In spite of the dark I detected the presence of that slimy, gigantic leper who seems ready to attack the city. The low and irregular houses were like bubbles on a marsh. Country of stray dogs, the suburb exhibited its pustules, as a prostitute her pox.

The night clung to the trees, then, lying in wait in the shadowy spaces or crouching in the long, narrow and somber streets, it seemed to spy upon us as if we were emerging from some dive. The least noise was a catastrophe, the least breath a great terror. We walked in the eternal mud. Step by step we sank into the thickness of night, lost as if forever. I turned around several times to look at the way we had come but night alone was behind us. When we came upon a small light in a dead house, instantly it went out, as if frightened by our passing.

All at once a fresh breeze welcomed us, and the night became more beautiful, larger, more itself. We arrived at the banks of the Seine.

Indefatigable, Octave crossed a bridge, followed by my fatigue and my tenacity. On the bridge, the wind began to grumble. Octave turned sharply to the left and for several minutes followed the deserted quays. His shadow, jostled from time to time by the light of a street lamp, galloped about him. He stopped at last before a sort of shed and pushed open its door with a shove of his shoulder. I drew near and heard a noise like tin cans being thrown to the ground. I was spying upon I knew not whom. I hoped for I know not what. At the end of a short time, it is true, I lost patience, my imagination having assured me that Octave was asleep at last.

I returned on my steps; I was completely exhausted. Near the bridge was a café, before which a bench offered itself to my fatigue. I sat down without thinking that any other decision could be possible. Dawn was beginning and I was present at the awakening of this pitiful suburb, like a corpse rotting at the edge of the Seine.

As the night receded everything began to move. Long streams of light sprang from the earth and, gaining the sky, swept the clouds. Day slowly began to sprout.

In spite of my empty head, my eyes were sharp as points and I lost none of dawn's gestures. My thoughts continued to follow Octave; he was moving away from me more and more rapidly, diminishing in my mind's eye. His countenance, which now and then appeared to me, was sometimes changed into that of his sister, who would rise before me. Faithful and faithless, at the same time, she was overawing. I felt that she was not the same since I had learned that she could be Georgette of the day and Georgette of the night, that two women, as different from each other as darkness and light, dwelt in that pale and supple body, that shadow dressed in black. She seemed to attract mystery as water attracts the light. About her danced I know not what cold and inviting flame. Georgette possessed the charm of the invisible.

Since our first meeting in the place Saint-Germain-des Prés, she had taken part in every event possessing an element of strangeness at which I had been present. She was at once the witness and the cause of this incomprehensible succession of mysteries. It is she, said I to myself, who holds the key to the incomprehensible and yet she forgets that I cannot understand what to her appears so simple. Chance was playing with me but not with her. And I could not grasp what it was that tied her to certainty, clarity, and truth.

Invisible, she nevertheless came and went, traversing this mystery without fears or regrets.

And he who was her brother had suddenly become a part of it. It was not like Octave to amuse himself by interfering in the game, but—because of Georgette, I imagined—his proceedings were difficult to reconcile.

Near me, no doubt, he was now sleeping and I tried to vision that shed as having no other reason to exist than to affect reality in some way or other.

Quite as a matter of course everything began to grow strange. My enemy, that particular morning, was chance, which permitted me no respite.

Chance, said I to myself, is at least sincere in that it does not conceal its deceptions from us. On the contrary it exposes them in broad daylight, and trumpets them at night. It amuses itself, from time to time, by stupefying the world with the shock of a terrible surprise, as if to remind men of its great strength, thinking they might forget its flightiness, its mischief, its whimsicalities. The complacencies of chance are not favors but treacheries: it does not amaze us save to keep us in its grasp and all that we receive from its hands are not so much gifts it is offering us as pledges we make to remain its slaves in perpetuity, subject to the grievous visitations of its harsh and malicious power.

Inadvertently paraphrasing a famous text, I bowed my head before defeat and resigned myself no more to struggle with this fate which had suddenly seized me.

What made it possible for me not to abase myself utterly was the tenderness of Paris which I saw from afar slowly mounting above the shadows and following the sun in its course. A sharp wind arose, a signal for the general awakening.

Autos leaped into being, throwing into my face their speed and their clatter. Shutters rattled and the café which sheltered me opened at last.

When the first street car appeared, I got up and my legs were barely able to carry me. I was boarding the car with difficulty when I saw someone running at full speed and signaling to the motorman to wait a few seconds. I admired the runner; Octave leaped into the car which was waiting for him alone.

He installed himself in second class and started to examine his fingers, moving them thoughtfully.

For a minute or two I had the desire to throw myself upon him, to slap him and beat him. His calmness appalled me. He seemed so much at ease, so assured, so absorbed in his occupation that he insulted my weariness, my frayed nerves, my distraught mind.

I remembered Octave's strange habits, which his sister had described, his experimental hobbies, and came once more to doubt his sanity.

At the terminus he jumped lightly from the car and walked toward a watchmaker's shop. There he stopped dead, standing for a long time examining either the watches or the clocks, first one and then another. I couldn't keep it up and abandoned his trail. Inspired by a singular hope, I threw myself upon the newspapers for an explanation. But I read there only of occurrrences similar to that which I had observed, similar but not the same and they seemed to me so pale, so discrete, that I cast aside the paper with a sort of disgust.

CHAPTER SEVEN

I had no fear of forgetting. Slowly spring approaches. The sky seems younger, and the clouds frolic like children.

One day it was announced that the race course at Longchamps was about to open its gates. At this time I was no longer thinking of them, those people whose names I feared to pronounce. They had disappeared, I hoped, and everything was blotted out. Paris swelled with light, the nights grew shorter.

I went, as I did each year, to see the races, again to breathe in the intoxication of the open air. I was sure to see again the faces of the faithful, to observe the anguish of others. It was an official ritual that one celebrated. All of these friends of one afternoon, my Longchamps friends, were in love with chance. They awaited it with impatience, relied upon it. Everyone was smiling.

I took a slow turn about the stands and on the course, around the baskets of flowers, relived my memories and rediscovered men, all of us quite amazed to find one another still alive. The common herd, so called, were just the same, menacing and gay, sensitive and cruel. A piece of Paris.

The races begin, I lose and in a little while decide to "change my luck" by going out on the paddock to take a chance there at winning.

Near the wickets old men were in the majority and I marveled at the perpetuity of hope.

All the dealers were at their posts and to amuse myself I went to see them sell their merchandise. And there, to my great surprise what should I see but Octave, selling inside tips! He was shouting I don't now what sort of formula designed to attract customers and his shouts were so monotonous that in listening to him one thought more of a song than of an appeal. His eyes fixed on the skies, he was a dealer in chance. An angry and suspicious loser demanded the return of the money which he had put up hoping to win. But Octave heard nothing.

I drew near and he recognized me in short order. Then he handed me a small paper and I paid. He barely thanked me and continued his recital. But I didn't let him off with that and asked him a few questions. He answered with bad grace. Not far off, his neighbor, the friend in the slouch hat, offered to buy back the winning tickets from those who were impatient. But the two confederates put so little zest into their business that I saw at once these noisy occupations were no more than alibis. The winks they gave prospective clients removed my last doubts. Octave and his pal were purely and simply bookmakers. With admiration I watched them playing the rôle they had chosen for themselves and I was astonished at the hypocrisy of Octave, who was lost in his dreams. Astonishment is decidedly contagious for, turning my head, I saw that in turn a man seemed surprised at my amazement and was observing me with a smile. When his look met mine he approached me and asked point-blank: "Do you know William?"—designating Octave. Though taken aback by the given name, I replied:

"Yes, certainly."

"What a guy!"

My new friend was frankly amused by the thought of Octave and the joy he was about to experience in telling me some anecdotes. My interlocutor was a babbler, one of those men who take you by the button of your jacket and punctuate their discourse with "Old man", "Am I right?" "Unbelievable" and other locutions of the sort.

"You ought to see him," said he to me, "on one of his good days. In general he is a silent lad, but when it gets him, you've got to take your hat off. I, who am talking to you, I knew him in the Reserves. One day he told the sergeant that he wanted to try some experiments and at supper he dropped several plates on the floor to hear the noise it would make. To shut him up, some of his friends gave him a few swift kicks. 'All right, let him go ahead, I should worry.' Some boob for a joke told him that he had drunk his urine and that it was better than water. What should he do but go try it to find out the taste."

The other continued to spin out his recital of the experiments of him whom he called William, but under pretext of going to play my four bits I left him, very sure that he would choose from among the deeds and acts of Octave only those which seemed to him really amusing, or to be exact, excrementitious.

William-Octave, throughout the narration of his regimental comrade, appeared to me the same as he whom his sister had described to me at the time of my first visit. That mania for experiments, that absent look which immobilized his face, and that obstinacy in pursuing his course marked the character of this strange fellow, this vagrant of Paris, one of those eternal loiterers who haunt the streets, with haggard eyes and hands in their pockets.

Octave went his way, jostled about yet preoccupied. He was one of those of whom it is said: "Where are they headed to?" I never could guess his destination. He lived in the midst of us like a street light.

When the result of the last race had been posted, as if he were passionately interested Octave moved near the wickets and offered to buy up the winning tickets of those standing in line. In vain.

I took my eyes off this friend and he lost no time in disappearing in the crowd.

That same day, on my way home, in front of the Gare d'Orsay I chanced upon someone else. It was the sailor who had followed me on that memorable night. He was now hanging around the passengers, still carrying his enormous canvas sack, waiting for I don't know what. With an uneasy air he was watching the few travelers, who come and go in railway stations like animals in a trap.

I remembered having heard a lengthy discussion of him at the conference in the aquarium of the Trocadéro and also recalled that talkative young man, too talkative to be frank, who had commented upon the drama of the man who had been cut to pieces. This vagabond sailor, then, was no more than the common fugitive assassin for whom the police were searching.

I don't know what feeling impelled me to circle about him in my turn, seeking to have a word with him. He could, at least if he wanted, aid me to understand the amazing vagaries of chance.

Finding him at the very place where I had made his acquaintance, I was persuaded that this coincidence had a considerable importance. I knew that places and environment have a profound influence on memory and the imagination, and I hoped, that night, to find the password of the enigma.

I relied on Paris, on the night and on the wind. I expected much of the Gare d'Orsay where one may occasionally hope and wait without aim or reason. The two twin clocks pointed to the hour of one; on the Seine, the reflections of fires and lights were still dancing by, like a galloping flock. The sky at this hour was black and menacing. Spring was not yet the master, and night escaped his power.

The silence spread minute by minute, besieging the station from which the last employees were now escaping. The sailor alone resisted and kept walking from the baggage room to the gate, ever on the alert. He kept his head bent in the manner of impatient horses who paw the ground with their hoofs.

I thought it likely that he hadn't a sou and was looking for a cigarette or a drink. A nameless beggar, he was lugging his far too heavy burden over the station pavement. I counted also on the peculiar craving of murderers to talk of their crime and to boast of their cruelty. It was a willing ear that he sought, no doubt, and being convinced as to his frame of mind, of that which psychologists call his state of soul, I stepped up to him.

The sailor, of course, did not recognize the one who a few months before had graciously offered him a cigarette. He looked at me naïvely, astonished no doubt by this quiet passer-by, who most obviously seemed out for a stroll, and was not to be taken for a traveler.

"Have you a light?" said I, showing my unlit cigarette.

"Neither light, nor tobacco."

I offered him a cigarette.

We soon decided to leave the station in order to find a passing smoker or a café still open.

"Do you know of a bistro?" I asked, to continue our conversation.

He grunted to avow his ignorance.

"Let's take a look around."

While we were walking toward the Institute, I tried several times to talk to the sailor. It was useless. He did not even open his mouth to answer me, being content to grunt or to shake his head. When we passed near a street lamp and its light would strike his face, I quickly observed him, trying to guess what he was thinking. He seemed, above all, hesitant and perplexed. In his half-closed eyes was a look of anxiety. But he sucked his unlighted cigarette with so evident a pleasure that I was loath to believe him preoccupied. From street lamp to street lamp I came finally to understand that what annoyed and disturbed him was probably lack of money.

He was following me faithfully, first because he had nothing better to do, and also because he hoped for a handout into the bargain.

We were drawing near to the Institute and as soon as we made out its shadow I staked all on one throw.

"Do you know Georgette?"

In the most natural way in the world he answered:

"The little brunette?"

It was little enough to go by, but the tone with which he replied left me no doubt. The sailor knew Georgette well.

I suggested resting on the steps of the Pont des Arts. We gazed at the Institute and its lacy shadows. Did he know that he had been betrayed in this place? And what is more, was it he whom they had betrayed?

The sailor had put down his sack and like those used to long watching, he rested his elbows on his knees and pressed his hands against his chin. He seemed to be looking attentively at the stairs and the railings. His gaze went from the statue of the Republic to those stone lions who seem to be laughing as they keep watch.

A faulty gas jet was whistling full blast and only the wind gusts could make it stop. The sailor was not meditating, but observing the changes night brought about in this place. I should have liked to read these signs of destiny with him, but he kept in his shell. He looked at everything about him from a great distance and without the least fear. Whereas the recollection of those tragicomic scenes which had unfolded themselves before my eyes filled me with a sort of drunkenness amounting almost to vertigo, he was as calm as if days and nights still lay between us and these banks of the Seine, this somber place where his life had been at stake. For, henceforth, I could not for an instant think that the sailor-assassin, the murderer betrayed by the woman with the bundle after she had been worked upon by the tragic stage setting, was other than the man seated next to me at the verge of day.

A taxi, the same kind as that other which had crossed this square at an unseasonable hour, passed at top speed as was the custom here. That exact detail precipitated a decision in me.

"A few months back," said I, offering my neighbor a cigarette, "I was walking by here with a girl and we stopped a moment on the sidewalk you see over there at the corner of the street. A few seconds after our arrival, we saw a big car pull up and an unheard-of number of people came from every side and stood around the man who had jumped from the auto.

"We heard screams and a woman dropped to her knees, clasping her hands. Weeping, she began to speak and fell at last full length upon the ground. Immediately all these sinister individuals left, and it was not until the next day, in the papers, that I found the probable explanation of this scene, reading that a woman had betrayed the murderer of the man who had been cut to pieces and found near the Pont-Neuf. The murderer was her lover, a sailor. Are you the sailor?"

I put the question to him brutally. Then:

"Are you a policeman?" he asked me.

And when, with a good deal of force, I had answered no, he looked at me quietly and attentively and said:

"Yes, I'm the one."

Then he stopped. I didn't know how to take up the thread of my discourse and I waited for him to yield to the need of telling his crime.

I waited a long time before he opened his mouth. He kept gazing at the steps of the Institute with the same faraway look.

"She couldn't do anything else," said he aloud at last and as if speaking to himself.

"Why did she let it out?"

"The man in the car, that's Volpe. He thinks he's all-powerful because he's an amateur policeman and journalist. He wants to prove, he says, that the police don't know their job and that he is able to unearth murderers quicker than any of the inspectors. He suspected something when he saw Marie rambling about and he drew her into a trap. She's a bit of a coward and she thought that everything Volpe told her was true, that they were going to guillotine her. . . .

"But all the same Volpe didn't dare write my name in his paper. He let it go at that. Besides, he's satisfied because he found out who was the murderer. He'll write a book about it. Idiot."

I only partially understood his explanations; the strange personage called Volpe seemed to me to be a somewhat specialized dilettante. I had heard speak of him vaguely and knew only that he was one of those people called fire buffs, one of those who pay the clerks of the department a good sum to be notified immediately when a fire has broken out. They rush to the scene of the disaster and feast upon the sight.

I had also been told that this Volpe frequented certainly highly specialized houses, where one may, for a relatively modest sum, enjoy certain strange sights.

Volpe was a man of legend, at once celebrated and un-known, one of those, so numerous in Paris, who is never mentioned but whose reputation is nevertheless well established. Often the legend is based on nothing at all, but occasionally it is only a very pale reflection of the reality.

The sailor continued to develop arguments the logic of which more often than not escaped me. I caught several tags of phrases but as a matter of fact I was trying especially to piece together the strange adventure of the Institute, with the aid of several words more clear than the rest.

I well knew that Paris is a city dark and full of mysteries, that the men who haunt it are often creatures in hiding, tracked or lost, but I had not believed it really possible thus to escape the power of all those laws which constantly threaten innocents like me. I seemed to forget the night, but suddenly I called to mind long solitary walks during which it would have been possible for me to commit the most irregular acts without drawing attention. And to give myself immediate proof of it: I was surprised that no one seemed to be concerned with the singular posture of the two of us, the sailor and I, seated on the steps of the Pont des Arts.

Everything breathed of peace, and silence ruled absolute. No passer-by came to disturb our dialogue. There were in Paris so many other dogs to whip, less gracious, in appearance at least, than we.

Straining my ears, waiting for every word that would have any meaning to me, I let the sailor do the talking. He continued to argue with himself, to weigh the pros and cons, criticizing the aforementioned Marie or himself.

He spoke of this woman quite simply, but with a great love. He said that she was nervous but good. Never did he deliberately use a word or a locution in slang to express himself; when he departed from the habitual language, he did it so naturally and with such spontaneity that I saw at once he knew no other terms, or else he had forgotten them.

Through these mists which he could not scatter I perceived that he was profoundly attached to this Marie, but that he was suffering from a kind of jealousy. She earned her living by prostituting herself and during the sailor's absence had placed herself under the protection of another man.

The sailor decided to put an end to this situation and had killed him.

"Naturally," I put in at this moment. "But why did you give yourself the trouble to cut him to pieces?"

"I never gave it a thought," said he. "I didn't know how to get rid of him and the idea came to me to dump him in the Seine. Then Octave told me that I should first cut him into pieces."

Hearing that name I gave a little start but the sailor continued:

"Too difficult. But the idea gripped me. I'd revenge myself better. The bastard—I was going away but I came back to look him over. He was still staring with his glassy eyes. I couldn't resist. When I had finished, the sweat was pouring off me. I wrapped the whole thing in a cloth and threw it over there."

He extended his arm in the direction of Notre-Dame.

"They found it later on near the bridge. I don't know how."

His intervals of silence became longer, until he ended by grumbling to himself. I asked him then:

"And Octave?"

"Always the same," said he, "with his ideas. He's a great guy. I saw him again the other day. I don't know what he's been up to, that fellow. He can't rest in peace any more. He's parading about all the time, day and night. Georgette follows him, but he goes faster than she does. And then there's the spying. He'll end by doing some mischief."

"But how did you manage to keep from being caught?"

"To begin with, they're afraid of me. No one will give me away. Then they're too stupid. I have no home, you know. I've finished my time six months ago now, they don't know what's become of me. They don't know me. I go out only at night."

This time he stopped. Either from prudence or weariness, I don't know which.

He remained awhile longer, seated on the steps of the bridge, lost in an endless reverie, figuring out his schemes.

Before leaving him I thought it would be best to give him some money, so that he would not regret his confidences. He accepted in the simplest possible manner and said to me amiably:

"Thanks, buddy."

CHAPTER EIGHT

After my conversation with the calmest of assassins it seemed easy to unroll the thread of what I had been calling a mystery. I even confess that I could not help feeling a kind of disappointment, when I thought over the manner, at the same time too simple and too artful, in which I had obtained the clues. The sole being in all this gang who still held a charm for me was this Volpe. I busied myself with gathering further facts about him. I was anxious to see him.

The first idea that came to me was to ask Georgette for exact details, but I soon realized that she knew nothing or next to nothing, or else, in all probability what intrigued me or appeared strange to me was for her no more than one of many similar episodes in her life. Assuming that she had retained the least remembrance of the incident, or noticed its occurrence, she could undoubtedly have told me any number of stories of the sort.

She would have answered my questions:

"Well, what about it? That's Paris."

She would have been a thousand times right. It was Paris which I thought I knew and of whose sex and mystery I was ignorant, it was Paris unrecognized and rediscovered, the breath and gestures of Paris, Paris and her supple and silent nights—Paris and her folds, Paris and her faces.

It was Volpe that I had to see and that I did see. Volpe, of course, is not his name. He goes by so many names that it's not known whether he really has one. It is Louis Dubois, alias ——, alias ——, alias ——, alias ——, etc. He needs names for alibis, since for him all trades are fruitful.

Generally despised, Volpe is strong enough to make use of the contempt with which they surround him. I knew that he was interested in a newspaper and that he was chief of a gang of bookmakers, that he traded on the Bourse and was connected with the music hall game, that he was at the same time friend and terror of prostitutes, that he owned a small house in Neuilly and had a furnished room in Charentonneau, that he had an auto and that he went about at night in company with white slavers like himself.

It was impossible to number Volpe's occupations since his main object was to make as much money as possible in the briefest time possible.

Not long after this I was shown a fat, short-winded individual in front of a café in the rue Royale, with baggy eyelids, a hanging lower lip, big red hands hairy and decorated with rings. He was dressed with a certain elegance and yet insignificant details somehow betrayed vulgarity. He carried himself well. His look was at the same time direct and hypocritical, but that look was a power in itself. Under thick bushy eyebrows, the pupils of his eyes would suddenly become fixed and then his glance would be so firm that nothing could deflect it. Impossible not to think of an arrow. I was seated not far from him and I heard him discussing some sort of paper pulp business. He was "tutoying" his adversary and one felt that this mode of speech came naturally to him, also his heavy and insulting laugh, his too precise gestures.

Abruptly he took his hat off to fan himself and his pointed bald head came to light. There one could best discern his strength. The nape of his neck was really imposing, that of a man not easily intimidated.

He stood up brusquely and hailed a taxi.

"Gare Saint-Lazare, boy, and shake it up," he ordered the chauffeur. The door slammed. Volpe stretched himself out on the cushions.

Then, for several days, I didn't see him again. One of Volpe's strengths is that he has no habits. He is mobile and sure of himself.

My wish must have been stronger than I suspected, for I waited no more than a few days to be introduced to this singular person whose active influence over the destiny of many beings I had gradually discovered, almost by accident—these beings who suddenly, before my eyes, had come to represent Paris and its merciless night.

Volpe was very amiable and spoke to me at once of a thousand insignificant things which he loosed like so many insects. I looked at him without listening, with that persistence and that impertinence which go with curiosity.

Volpe was still uglier when examined close up. His thick skin formed uneven folds about his mouth whose flabby lips were of a purple tinge. A mollusk face. There was in Volpe's manner I can't tell what mechanism which proclaimed the systematized habit of throwing one off the scent. His amiability and his "good fellow" attitude were irritating beyond all words, when one wasn't fooled by them.

He was accompanied that night by a short stout man, almost clothed by his beard—one saw only this thicket of hair—who held a cigarette he had just lit. Hands behind his back, stomach protruding, his silhouette made you think of a dictionary.

We soon left the servants' ball where we had met. These diverting weekly dances have the charm of monkey cages. The valet does courtesy to the cook out for a good time.

Volpe, who came to these reunions for interests of his own, knew how to be amused nevertheless by these imitations.

The walking dictionary told us, with corroborative quotations, of the singular habits of servants. He described to us with many details the check room for small children, who were deposited under a number by nursery girls. This custom, he affirmed with a disarming certainty, is very ancient. And he cited cases of substitution of children infinitely more numerous than one would suppose. Now and then he underlined what he said with an observation borrowed from Restif de la Bretonne, who was plainly his model. Volpe let him talk.

Every incident was the occasion for a lecture from the little old man. When, on the boulevard, Volpe left us, giving us to understand with all the vulgarity one could wish the motive for his isolation, he whom I compared to a dictionary plucked me by the sleeve and offered me something like this:

"These public conveniences are decidedly ugly," he began. "But they are more practical than anything that had been invented before them. Do you know," said he, smiling in his best manner, "that toward the end of the middle ages, bucket carriers circulated through the streets to give aid to people who were 'caught short'? They were armed with a great cloak forming a sort of temporary shelter from which emerged the face alone of the crouching client. After which the bucket was emptied into the nearest stream.

"In the eighteenth century, this primitive shelter was re-placed by a sort of open-bottomed chair mounted on four wheels. In sum, a rolling privy.

"The police regulations forbade the 'concession holders' to remain at a standstill once they had 'taken on' a client. The man had to set out walking as chance might lead, or, at least as I like to believe, in the direction the client had indicated. It would save the client so much time. History does not say whether the conductor walked, trotted or went at a gallop, but imagine, I beg of you, what our streets must have been like at this epoch. Under Louis XIII, only the half of Paris was paved; the ground was uneven, soft, boggy, full of quagmires or of heaps of rubbish and filth.

"When the filth became cumbersome, they heaped it up at designated places and these public dumps came finally to form small hillocks. In this way the butte Saint-Roch was built up, through which the elegant avenue de l'Opéra was cut.

"In the eighteenth century, shelters were arranged, principally along the quays—with no supervision or upkeep—and the corners of walls were the embryos of our first 'comfort stations.' "

Having finished his little discourse, now extremely satisfied with himself, the little old man fiddled around in his pocket and pulled out a sticky-looking cigarette which he soon lighted.

Volpe looked at him as one observes a laborer working at his job. He viewed him with indulgence, for the old fellow was teaching him a series of stories he could make use of.

I understood at once in observing Volpe that he knew to perfection how to make use of whoever might approach him. He would never let the conversation wander and sought always to give it the direction he desired. When he was tired of the purring he had unleashed, he cut the discourse short and turned to some other occupation.

"Good-bye, old chap," said he to the talker. "I'll see you again one of these days."

He shook the little old man by the hand and seizing my arm turned his back on him abruptly, leaving the other with a word still in his mouth.

He was not slow in questioning me. Volpe was never afraid of "putting his foot in it". He was one of those of whom it is said they don't travel by four roads. So in reference to Volpe the litany of expressions made to the measure of energetic and authoritative men could well be used.

"Ah! Ah! So you know my friend Octave."

I admired the audacity of this man who at the first stroke answered my unasked question.

I was wrong to play at being as smart as he by replying:

"Yes, I know Octave, and also Georgette and even the sailor."

Volpe doesn't like to have one fight with the same weapons

as he. He counted, by his sharp and precise question, on having me talk of Octave and leading me little by little to tell him of my meeting with his "friends", for he was much more concerned with knowing the details than in admissions of facts which he probably already knew. Perhaps he wanted to check up on the information of those who, wrongly or rightly, he considered his agents.

"I know," he came back with a satisfied air, "we're going to meet them presently."

Then Volpe, having decided to compel silence, walked along whistling to himself like those who follow their way along country roads chewing a straw. He twirled his too-richly ornamented cane.

They were waiting for him at the little café where Octave had taken me one night to find his friend the bookie. There were three or four of them holding a discussion under Octave's distant gaze.

Volpe shook hands rapidly with just the right aloofness. He seemed, one couldn't say why, to consider all these men as inferiors and to be doing them a signal favor in allowing himself to mix with them.

Volpe didn't like to lose his time and at once began a discussion of which the general outline escaped me. I thought it had to do with an important stake, of putting up a margin, of a caution to be observed.

Names and surnames flew like flies.

Suddenly there entered two men whom I knew by sight. They were habitués of the Montparnasse cafés. Every day they could be seen in front of the Dôme gesticulating and watching the comings and goings of the celebrated women of that little world. Sometimes one of them would start a noisy quarrel which rapidly changed to blows.

The most determined was one named Verbaut whose red apoplectic face could be easily recognized. He entered our café with a smile of defiance and at once accosted Volpe.

"You're the one I've been looking for," said he.

Volpe looked him full in the face.

"Have you something of importance to tell me today?"

He put a stress at once serious and ironical on the word today.

"Useless to try that game," said Verbaut sharply. "I came here to tell you to leave Georgette alone. I'm the one you'll have to deal with if you don't take this tip."

"Listen, Verbaut," replied Volpe in a calm, irritating tone of voice, "listen, my friend, I've told you already that I take no orders from you."

Verbaut tightened his lips and his fists; then, going close to Volpe's face, he yelled at him:

"I tell you for the last time to lay off of Georgette and to quit forcing that fool itinerary on her. She can earn her bit just as well in Montparnasse or elsewhere."

Verbaut lost ground by arguing the question; at this moment the others joined in and gave their opinion.

Volpe didn't listen to them. It seemed as if all this didn't concern him.

Octave, silent as always, looked at Verbaut now and then with undisguised astonishment. The latter had taken a place at our table and quite close to me. Now and again he would call me to witness and declared to me that this situation was intolerable, that this assault upon liberty was unjustifiable. He rigorously affirmed Georgette's good faith.

I thought of her following her way, carving her regular path through the night.

Reinforcements came to Verbaut in the persons of two poorly dressed young men armed with canes. They came up with determined steps, as if obeying an order.

"Well," said they to Volpe, "do you understand?" But Volpe turned to speak to Octave, silent as ever.

I took note that, in spite of the unanimous disapproval

which surrounded Volpe, those about the tables divided themselves into two distinct groups: one composed of Verbaut and his friends, the other made up of the companions of Octave. These latter, while not sharing Volpe's point of view, backed him up solidly. But all were ready to argue till the crack of dawn.

CHAPTER NINE

A something or other that has no name in any language.

—Tertullian

At the height of the discussion, Octave nonchalantly withdrew and made for the door. But this departure had not escaped Volpe who made me a sign underlined with a smile.

He took abrupt leave of the company, after his manner, and started in pursuit of Octave who nonchalantly as ever was walking along the quays. When he reached the place Saint-Michel we saw him turn sharply and follow the rails of car line No. 8 in the direction of the Gare de l'Est.

Octave, with all possible gravity and steadfastness, continued on his way without the least heed for us.

I asked Volpe, however, if he thought Octave was conscious of being followed.

"You don't know him yet. Nothing bothers him. And even if the whole quarter were at his heels he would continue his monotonous stroll just the same. Octave, without your suspecting it, is giving himself up to some experiment. I couldn't say what. That's just what I want to find out. What interests him nowadays is fire. Several months ago it was water which preoccupied him, then it was women. He would follow them sometimes day and night to observe them but without saying a word. He wanted to find out what would happen.

"If at this moment you accosted him and spoke to him about fire, he would doubtless stop and look at you disdainfully. He has his convictions. He does not abandon them, until he becomes interested in something else."

I had surprised in Volpe the weakness of the man: he was extremely vain. Happy because he could astonish me, he was inexhaustible on the subject of Octave. He wanted to say more as if anxious to relieve himself of a burden.

Octave plunged into the night, pursued by the great flamboyant beckonings of the high street lamps and by the murmur of Volpe's monologue.

Still wandering on these deserted boulevards were several women who, with bowed heads, came and went in search of the night's last thrills. Sleep froze the houses, now engulfed in silence, and mounted into the sky which paled at its approach. Not the slightest breath.

When Volpe stopped talking, I could hear the murmurs of sleeping Paris. Like a great ailing body, Paris turned and twisted to escape the fever's grip. But soon the calm renewed itself, like a flame poorly snuffed.

We drew near the Gare de l'Est. Still following the rails of the car line, Octave slanted to the right and went along the fence which surrounds the precinct of the administration buildings. With the same abruptness he leaped over and entered the yards close by the deserted tracks. We followed him through that confusion of rails. He stopped before a hill of coal, walked around it and, in the loving manner of a geologist, satisfied himself as to the nature of the heap. I recognized these gestures of Octave, at once crisp and careless, just as they had been at the time of my first pursuit.

Volpe, hidden in the shadow, watched him. A strong breeze came from the station lifting a cloud of coal dust. In the distance the terminal wore a holiday look. Octave, after having walked three or four times around the coal reserves, made his way cautiously toward the sheds where the locomotives under steam were waiting the hour of departure. He hesitated a little, fearing to be interrupted during his walk.

But when he saw the locomotive fires he put aside his fears and leaped toward the red circles.

He climbed into the first locomotive he came upon and, his hands behind his back, as if to see better, he stood motionless. However, on hearing a noise he quickly jumped and plunged into the night. He walked for a while, then stopped to watch the passing of a train whose lights formed a long serpentine of fire. He resumed his way as far as a group of gasometers. There were ten large black tanks that one might have thought to be the prey of giant serpents. Conscientiously, Octave made a turn about each of them, now and again striking one with a stone. While we were stealthily watching him, Volpe elevated his shoulders and motioned me to be silent. All of a sudden Octave started running to meet a wildcat locomotive, which driveled fire and smoke. We thought he was about to be crushed but, like a toreador, he nimbly avoided the locomotive which passed him with a sigh.

Octave stopped once more before an immense wall which

supported a building. The wall was tragic, black with smoke and dust, disgusting with posters all in shreds. But at the top it was pierced by a window still showing a light. It looked like a solitary eye in the night. Octave picked up a stone from the roadbed and, taking a swing, threw it as hard as he could in the direction of the window. The stone missed its aim and fell at our feet. Octave repeated the experiment several times without result, then all at once we heard a noise of broken glass and a flood of abusive language followed, echoing along the wall. Octave was already far off.

I asked Volpe what Octave was looking for but he motioned me to be silent, for the latter was coming toward us. He passed close to our hiding place, going toward the footbridge. He climbed the stairs which lead to the signals, observed for a few moments the lantern which lights them, then jumped down and regained the street. We hastened to follow the same path. Octave ran in zigzags before us like a boy selling papers.

Volpe had some difficulty in keeping that pace; he got out of breath but would not relinquish the pursuit.

He ordered a taxi to follow Octave who, indefatigable, ran faster and faster. On the place du Châtelet, Volpe or-

dered the chauffeur to speed up in order to outdistance
Octave, whereupon we jumped out of the taxi, to meet him.

When Octave saw Volpe before him, he stopped short
and gave a friendly nod.

Instead of questioning him as I should have done and as
I wanted to do, Volpe simply fell in step with him without
saying a word. Octave returned home and we accompanied
him to the door. Day was near and we could hear the rum-
bling that announces the end of the night.

On the threshold Octave seized Volpe by the arm and
gave him to understand that the time had come to keep silent.
He awaited I know not what, listened intently and opened
wide his eyes. Day became more and more distinct: every-
thing was mauve. When it grew cold, Octave said to us in
a low voice: "Soon now," then he went in. Volpe had the
anxious look of people who seek to comprehend. He did
not remove his eyes from the entryway through which Oc-
tave had just gone. A few shops came to life.

Instinctively I kept silent, leaving Volpe to his reflections.

A shadow approached us. Arms loaded with groceries,
Georgette of the day was walking along rapidly. When she
saw Volpe, she started like a frightened horse.

Volpe on seeing her did not move and Georgette passed before us, without even greeting us. I wanted to speak to her, but with a curt gesture he arrested my impulse.

Day, in establishing itself definitely in Paris, cast over all a cold drought which suggested the end of something. Volpe, still motionless, seemed to be waiting for someone but when the screeching milk wagons appeared at a gallop, Volpe lost all hope and patience.

He dragged me toward the boulevard Saint-Germain in search of a café and installed himself, in spite of the chill, at a small table outside. His elbows on the marble, he ate greedily. His large heavy eyes were closing.

When he had finished his generous breakfast, he asked me for a cigarette.

He ruminated for some time before yielding to a manifest desire to talk to me.

"Do you believe Georgette is wise to her brother's schemes?" I asked him.

"Georgette? Perhaps you think you know that woman. You'll never understand her, for you'll always think you must credit her with ideas and intentions.

"Georgette lives outside what we think of as her true self—you as well as I. For my part, I have never been able to admit that she is only one who passes, who obeys. Georgette is a woman. That's all I can say. She lives and that's all. You don't know the rôle she plays among all these people you have met in my company. You might compare it to that of a fetish or of a mascot."

Suddenly Volpe assumed a grave look.

"If she should ever disappear for one reason or another, what a mess. . . ."

The cold morning had given Volpe the only drunkenness of which he was capable.

"Tell me, when Georgette disappears, have you noticed that day is not far distant? If she should disappear forever, I have a feeling, and believe me I don't let things muddle me, I have a feeling there would be no more night."

Volpe got up and gave me to understand that he was leaving unaccompanied and that I was not to go with him.

I pondered, as I nibbled the last roll in the basket, on what Volpe had said to me and on that statement which was at once incomprehensible and final. Georgette is a woman.

So that's the way they explain the mystery. With that statement they think to explain all. I smiled skeptically and yet I myself could not help but be content with that explanation.

Slowly I went on my way, following the day's ascent. While the sun rose and came to greet me, I marveled at being able to live in the midst of mystery without being wonder-struck each second. I admitted that we grow accustomed to the strangest circumstances and smiled with pity thinking of those who refuse to be what is called dupes—who want to know everything and who are not even able to perceive the diurnal mystery which suffuses and bathes them from head to foot.

During this sunny early morning walk I saw chance grow big before my eyes. It appeared to me like a powerful but accessible person who assumes the guise of thousands of human beings. It was not only this peaceful passer-by coming toward me, but also that drunk and tired taxi driver; it was Volpe and Octave, it was perhaps part of myself. Still it grew, and after a moment I concluded that Paris, my city, was one of its favorite dwelling places. I was willing to believe that chance was universal but in Paris, more than elsewhere, I seemed to see it more easily, almost to touch it with the finger. It was, said I to myself, the hands of time.

The loud noises of morning and the strong odors of spring circled about me as if to vouch for my reasoning. These noises, these odors were the toys of chance, like so many other things, for chance plays without ceasing, and takes the lead. I knew well, forsooth, that there are men who wish to wrestle with it, others who deny its existence, but others who count on it alone. There are others who accept its orders simply, perhaps, without thought and that morning I wanted to be like these last, who seemed closer to me, and stronger.

I stopped on the Pont de la Concorde and looked with enjoyment at the elbow formed by the Seine. On the river floated a scum of objects, pieces of wood, nameless debris gliding to their destiny. Some of them, jumbled together, had taken refuge in a little bay. The current disturbed them, tossed them back ironically, and sometimes seized bits of them to toss them into the middle of the stream.

My eyes ran from one bank to the other.

Now my mind would stem the current, and now abandon itself to the flow. Now I wished to look for causes, for motives, and now I willingly accepted my ignorance, my simplicity.

In the distance, between the towers of Notre-Dame, I saw spring appearing. Then a wind arose, immense, and shook itself like the biggest flag I had ever in my life beheld.

CHAPTER TEN

There are months during which we live under one certain sign, be it that of misfortune, love or chance.

I did my best, during the days which followed my meeting with Volpe, to find once more the tracks of this personage and to know his habits. I was not unaware that Volpe is, after all, a relatively common type in Paris, that of the man who wants to get on and who will succeed in getting—legally or illegally, according to circumstances—the most money in the least time. Many of them are the heads of flourishing businesses, above or below board, where it must be acknowledged they show indisputable abilities. The most astonishing of these abilities is the one which helps them to a notable ascendance over people little inclined to submission. Volpe was of those able to command men who have a horror of obedience and whose lives are examples of perpetual revolt.

So it was that Volpe reigned over this special world to which an absence of scruples in conjunction with a remarkable initiative faculty represented the greatest power. It is a commonplace to say of a man that he manipulates certain of his fellows like pieces on a chessboard. This well-worn simile still seemed fresh to me when I thought of the manner in which Volpe made use of the different members of his circle.

Volpe had been, it seems, a dock hand at Bordeaux when he first thought to utilize his physical magnetism in a concert hall of that city. His fine figure caused him to be noticed by a certain woman who came often to the place, and they united their destinies. This woman owned two or three so-called special houses in Bordeaux which were a large source of revenue. When, according to one of his favorite expressions, he had made a pile, he came up to Paris and began his operations.

I could not find out the exact number of his occupations.

But prostitution, racing, gambling, the music hall and its branches interested him equally and brought him in enough. He was always ready to buy something and sell it again as quickly as possible and to the best advantage. One day he sold pictures, the next day cotton and in all probability women. He possessed blocks of shares in a number of newspapers, whose policy he controlled and which served him at the same time as buffers against the world. What struck one about Volpe was his remarkable gift for using to the hilt everything that belonged to him. He had the taste for small enterprises whose yields were prompt and it could be said that he enriched himself through makeshifts. Like all those in his category, Volpe had a great number of vices. But he loved best of all to dominate.

In the circle whose life I was witnessing, he stood the unquestioned master. And to keep that power he was capable of anything. The strange stage setting which he had organized one night before the Institute was just one of the tricks which were his custom. That spectacular bluff had permitted him to recapture his ascendancy. The woman who resisted him, who would not confess to him, who was in revolt, if he had not compelled her by no matter what means to obey, would have been the most grievous example for the whole band. He could not permit them to hide something from him. And he did not permit it.

Undoubtedly, he would not have been able to menace the sailor's mistress directly, to turn her over to the police, for he would immediately have been considered as a traitor or rather as a man not worthy of respect, but he wished to create a doubt. All that mobilization of forces, of suggestion, must have deeply impressed that woman who in spite of everything was always capable of weeping at a melodrama and of crying out at the movies when a sympathetic character was strangled.

Volpe knew all this and he did not hesitate to organize the spectacle of which I had been a witness. Perhaps he was the first to laugh at it or to judge it far-fetched. But he knew better than anyone else the souls of those women who have no other counselors than cards, who firmly believe in the sorceries of the queen or the deuce of spades. Volpe himself consulted the cards or had them read for him. This man, who lived comfortably in the present, had a sincere dread of the future. He wished to seize it boldly, even though he suspected it was stronger than he, but he could not admit the terrible mist of tomorrow. From a certain point of view Volpe was a gambler and, like all that race, he was superstitious, sensitive to omens, passionately in love with the future.

He knew himself well and this weakness, which he easily detected in others since he could recognize it, he utilized. When he learned the rôle the sailor was playing he had no thought, of course, of giving him up, but wished, on the contrary, to enroll him and from that day, he kept him under his protection.

None of those who knew, or had learned through Volpe, the name of the assassin would have thought of giving him up. First because of that oft-mentioned honor among thieves, then from hatred of the common enemy, finally through fear of Volpe who had on several occasions made it clear he had granted protection.

Pulling the wires, possessing the secret of all these lives, he dared permit himself to command. He did so permit it, but he also assured a livelihood to each. I often saw him approached and never saw him refuse. He had a familiar gesture which he repeated frequently before me. Bending forward, he thrust his left hand into the inner pocket of his jacket to take out his wallet which he opened quickly and from which he speedily extracted a bank note. And never did he ask the reason for the loan, never did he seek to be repaid. Many of those whom he directed were sincerely devoted to him, first because they feared and admired him and then because they knew that to struggle was useless. Others however plainly hated him. Octave's friend, the man in the slouch hat, was among the most hostile. He prowled about him like a vicious dog. He was, besides, an embittered man, like all who have fallen from their social stratum. He had been formerly the proprietor of a hotel, but the races, it was said, had ruined him. From gaming he had become a bookie. But he detested those who surrounded him and especially Octave whom he called his friend, but whom he loved to annoy with thoughtless proposals. He invented terrifying stories for Georgette's brother, incredible machinations. Really the most striking thing about all these people was their incredible love for the extraordinary. They had to feel that they were exposed to the most extravagant dangers. They saw enemies in all whom they did not know.

The man in the soft hat furnished magnificent stuff to these famishing imaginations. It was he who found and imposed meeting places as strange as the aquarium of the Trocadéro. And all took pleasure in the most bizarre spots. Gradually I understood, moreover, that this love of the strange was instinctive: they endeavored one way or another and as often as possible to subjugate their nerves, to scoff at the habitual and to sharpen their wits under all circumstances. And Volpe himself felt that same need for the fantastic.

I was astonished, amazed at the correlation between their imaginations and their life—"always full of surprises." These men who were forced to and loved to hide when they committed a deed could not escape from this deception. They had all acquired the habit of inventing, of deceiving, of preparing false trails, alibis of every sort.

The women who were their companions and on whom they lived remained for the most part outside of these imaginings. They had a recognized and accepted occupation, and they did not seek to dissemble. They submitted willingly to orders given, or even to brutality. They seemed happy to accept the life dictated to them.

Georgette occupied a place apart. She was the protégée of Volpe who, however, was not her lover. But this protection would not have sufficed to assure him that supremacy which all accorded him. She took part, to be sure, in their deliberations, she had her word to say, she was independent and, in a way, was treated like a man. The women did not consider her as one of their number. For Georgette was mystery to them all. The life she led was so sharply divided that it created illusion. Georgette of the day, Georgette of the night.

But at bottom all her prestige came from her aloofness and her independence. No one knew whence she came and none could explain the reasons for her association with this group. She accepted the ritual, the authority of Volpe, but only because she was quite satisfied to do so. During her absence they often discussed her attitude, they deplored the mystery which surrounded her will and her desires; they rejoiced in her versatility.

Georgette possessed a charm to which it was impossible not to succumb. When she went to Montparnasse early in the evening and Verbaut and the others grouped themselves about her, she still maintained this supremacy. They, who had only contempt and irony for the women with whom they surrounded themselves, accepted her air of indifference, her independence. They sought her presence.

Undoubtedly Georgette was pretty but more than one woman could have rivaled her. Her eyes, blacker than they appeared at first sight, rested upon things and people with a simplicity which rendered her look strange. When she spoke, a miracle occurred: her voice was sweet but somewhat husky, it undulated like a wraith of smoke, it insinuated, it was a murmur, but when Georgette's lips commenced to move, silence suddenly descended.

I do not remember having heard Georgette say anything definite, but when she spoke you were ready at once to believe and to follow her.

You loved her without quite loving her. She was feared a little, but above all you were uneasy as much because of her presence as her absence. She really needed no one.

Often they wondered why she kept watch over Octave, her brother, with so much care and precaution. And one imagined numberless reasons none of which bore examination.

About Octave were the same mists. He also was independent and they accorded him almost the same regard as they accorded his sister. They formed a mysterious couple which one admired, without confessing it, partially because of the mystery. Volpe's band, through all these common feelings, was exceptionally homogeneous and the group spirit was strong among them. None of them had other aim than to live without restraint. Dullness would seize them and to drive it off they sought mystery and created phantoms.

On leaving them I sometimes called them unachieved adventurers.

They plied trades often dangerous, but they were strictly professionals, possessing the same kinks and the same professional markings.

Among other corporate groups they held a place apart, *hors concours* if you will, but such as they were, they all remained upon the same level. Perhaps they might have been able to accomplish sensational thefts or commit notable crimes, but in that case they would have been just part of that Parisian army of which the reputation is universal.

They were adapted to their city and were henceforth a part of it like taxi drivers and lamplighters. It was useless for them to invent, even to create exceptional circumstances; they remained still Parisians with the hobbies and the habits of other inhabitants. Each was a reflection of Paris, a word in the refrain.

They willingly permitted themselves to be enslaved by the city, by it to be cradled. They loved it as they loved Georgette, with the same astonishment and the same submission. They could doubtless have circled the world, but they would have remained always the same, ties, habits, affections and hates, mixed.

One day, in a café—one of those cafés they love so much—I saw them listening with particular attention to a

refrain spit out by a gramophone: it was the hackneyed of
the hackneyed:

> *Paris, c'est une blonde*
> *Paris unique au monde.*

The imbecilic words spilled themselves before them and
they listened with open mouths, ravished, convinced.

CHAPTER ELEVEN

The days when we follow the secret voice of diversion are those chosen by chance to show us its ways.

Empty-handed, I set out upon the discovery of the flight of time and of space. Words, like joyous companions, started before my eyes and spun about my ears in a carnival of forgetfulness.

I was tired of those involuntary inquisitions, of those incessant curiosities. Boredom with the eternal pageant turned my thoughts to what you will. I fled voluptuously.

I had yielded to those boisterous beings who come to haunt me when I offer no opposition. That day at least three were making a disturbance. The savages would gladly have sung either hymns or music-hall refrains, but their greatest amusement consisted in carrying on a dialogue, one posing questions, the others replying in the most absurd way in the world. I was simply an ambulatory theater in which they were playing an improvised comedy, sister of the most persistent dreams. They were leading me I don't know where, intermixing times, places and sensations.

I arrived I don't know how on the heights which dominate Paris, at Bellevue.

The three accomplices, perceiving the panorama of the city which burst forth all at once, could not hold themselves for joy. Was it that bells were ringing? Were beacons of joy being kindled? I could not have denied this truthfully.

I no longer thought of silencing them. I thought only of listening.

"Paris," they cried, "spreads herself like the sun and the sun is a spot of oil. She consumes that which surrounds her as might the greatest conflagration of the century for she loves to wrap herself in the flames of her song, as all bells of the world know how to do at certain seasons."

What did they not give vent to in order to describe Paris

from whom I could no more remove my eyes than from a pool of water flaming with the sun! She seemed a mirror, an organ, a tree, she was anything you might desire with a quite unparalleled virtuosity. The three idiots quivered with excitement and lavishly compared the silhouette and shadow of the city with all manner of shapes, with all things that traversed my memory.

Before that turgid horizon thoughts emerged like bubbles and burst beneath the fire of that celebrated flame. I also saw spread out before me all the episodes of that year; the whole chain of days and faces unfolded. On that length of chart I sought the places and the beings I had known, that I had thought to know, as if they were forgotten archipelagos.

It was the "blue" café which I thought to locate first, then the Institute, the Trocadéro. . . .

This and all the rest revolved in my head, but I was thoroughly incapable of directing it.

While considering this panorama of time and of space, I was seized by a great lassitude. I wanted to laugh at myself and at the others. Come now, it was just a background more spacious than most and mechanical figures who gave me the illusion of living. From this distance, and retreating further into time, Octave, Georgette, Volpe, the sailor, were no more than painted wooden figures. Perhaps if I had looked into a mirror at that moment I should have succeeded in convincing myself that I, too, was no more than one of these figures. Little by little, however, in spite of all these circumstances, I felt the need to plunge again into that atmosphere.

And now to regain Paris that I thought to have lost.

I took the road back, abandoning my savages one at a time, in order to find again those resolute men who brush aside hesitations and pros and cons.

To my confusion, all that alienated me from them was just as clear to me as all that drew me toward them. But I remained convinced that those meetings had not been for nothing, that, without being clearly aware of it, for some time I had wished to find again those beings whose strengths and weaknesses had so astonished me.

Octave's perambulations might appear the whims of a sick person, Georgette's itinerary just professional, Volpe's actions not at all disinterested. But it was no less true that these explanations seemed to me really too simple. These lives possessed an inexplicable attraction which I called liberty. What mattered it, after all, that the occupations of each of them were of so simple a motivation, when a single gesture could demolish my whole logical structure?

Thus I felt that I had need of excuses. During these sallies of my spirit, they, for their part, had been content to live. Today perhaps Georgette would come across something she had no desire to seek, Volpe or Octave would lose confidence in their experiments.

They were in the right against me.

When night came and, following a habit which had become almost tyrannical, I had found some of them, I looked at them with different eyes. I could not, doubtless, call affection the sentiment which drew me toward them, but it seemed to me that it would take a catastrophe to separate me from or to disgust me with them, no matter how much I might wish it.

I envisioned this catastrophe as one foresees the end of a storm. They themselves were not ignorant of the fact that everything has an end and that one must eventually reconcile oneself to the inevitable. They ardently desired it.

This was probably why they so craved to know the future.

One of their principal occupations during their brief moments of idleness was to tell fortunes or to have others do it for them. The sailor's mistress, the weakest of the women, was adept in this art. Her great and unconscious skill consisted in announcing tragic events. She told them, in the most simple manner possible, what they all desired more or less to hear. Each urged her on to yield to this impulse repeatedly, to transfigure it, and the sorry words which she employed, almost always the same, acquired a grandeur which unbelievers can never know.

Hour on end they accepted this worn vocabulary which expressed their desires. They were not sated until they had begun to doubt, when they would murmur: "Isn't it too lovely?"

And when Marie had returned her filthy cards to her bag, there was a general discussion. They sought in the prophesied future a confirmation of the present.

When I came that night, Marie was telling Octave's fortune. She told him that soon he would accomplish great things.

The power of that weak and sluggish woman had she desired it would have been incomparable, but she had no inkling of such a thing. She alone, perhaps, could have vanquished Volpe, since he himself sought eagerly for what the cards might tell. He knew very well that she would never dream of really locking horns with him, but should she ever do so, he would not hesitate to crush her with dispatch, once and for all. This made me understand more clearly why Volpe in spite of opposition had marshaled all his strength, why he had extended himself to set his stage and play that drama worthy of the most out-of-date theater.

She lived now among them, retaining her power without using it, making herself the servant of all those whose passion is the future. As time passed, more and more did she become an instrument, a voice that speaks, what is called a medium.

About her clustered despairs.

Octave in harkening to her had believed that his destiny was henceforth fixed and from that moment forward he seemed to fear nothing. Henceforth he would trust himself to his life.

Volpe arrived presently. He remarked at once the strange expression to be read on Octave's face. About them, all remained silent. Volpe went up to Octave and asked:

"Where is Georgette?"

Octave shrugged his shoulders, replying: "You know perfectly well." For he no longer feared anyone and that name which, under all other circumstances, would have impressed her brother now seemed to make no impression on him.

We felt the need of waiting for someone or something, whom or what I do not know. A night sad and without fragrance. I was weary and bored with what I called the "doldrums", which no one any longer seemed to take seriously. When the sailor entered I had the feeling of an eternal renewal, the sensation of something that had happened before.

However, Octave on seeing the sailor went up to him and proposed that they go out. The other looked at his empty hands, at his sack lying in a corner, then without saying a word followed Octave. Volpe had not removed his eyes from them.

"Follow them," said he to the man in the soft hat.

Like a whipped dog, he who had been addressed arose and waited an instant or two looking through the window. Finally he went out.

Volpe had them tell him in minute detail what had happened. The laughing man, he who was so meticulous in the care of his beard, told him all that I had seen: Marie reading the future and predicting a better destiny for Octave. Volpe's heavy lip dropped; he closed one eye, listening to the bearded chap.

Marie hid herself, fearing Volpe's ire. From then on I had a clear idea that nothing would happen, that all this excitement, all these fears, were for nothing.

I recalled that long walk beyond the fortifications where I had freed myself of this band. Again I felt that disgust which follows curiosity assuaged. A movement of clockworks.

I quit the place myself as rapidly as possible. The streets seemed wholly unconcerned. No passer-by, no noise rose to disturb the night and provoke those waves whose ebb and flow I had followed for too many weeks. The entire city seemed to be frozen into absolute indifference. The street lamps and their plume of light were just simple gas jets, the porte-cochères were closed for good and all. The quarter lacked completely the nobility I had lent it.

To cap misfortune, shortly before I arrived at my lodging I met my old friend Jacques arm in arm with a woman.

When he saw me, he stopped short and raising his arms to the skies, cried out: "What has become of you? We never see you any more."

He introduced me to his lady friend, dragged me off to a night club, told me what he was doing, confided to me his latest impressions.

Thus he created the atmosphere of a world in which for some time I had ceased to live. Involuntarily I compared it with the one I had just quitted: taking in his lady friend, I thought of the women who followed Volpe.

The same disgust, the same weariness overcame me.

Paris, for Jacques and for them, played an incomprehensible rôle. It was the frame they preferred and I had the impression that they lived in an illusion.

I had seen it grow under my eyes whilst from Bellevue I considered the panorama. That great blot on the banks of the Seine again rotated on its axis just as did the whole earth, with the same persistence and the same resignation. Like the earth, Paris was growing cold and becoming simply an idea. For how many more years would she keep that power of illusion, for how many years would she live still mistress of time? I dared not answer. Watching the sticky night rain falling, I felt that everybody still wished to be deceived and to declare the perpetuity of his singular love.

Paris, the orchestra was probably singing, *est une* . . .

Everybody was dancing about me.

Suddenly I thought of that man who on looking at Rome said to me with perfect calmness:

"One civilization lost, ten regained."

Jacques was still speaking. My eyes closed, sleep and his sister indifference drew near.

There was nothing else for me to do but to take my leave.

CHAPTER TWELVE

Octave could hardly be alone in the café since he was talking with animation. He seemed to be addressing his remarks to a chair, but his gestures made it clear that he saw someone before him.

No one seemed astonished to see him conversing with emptiness. As for me, when he suddenly got up and went out of the café, I was surprised to see him abandon his place without taking leave of the invisible interlocutor.

He looked at me attentively and invited me to follow him, despite his habit. I offered no objection and we walked side by side and in silence for a good quarter of an hour. Octave knew where he was going.

He even seemed in a hurry.

He stopped on the quay near the Louvre and began to take observations.

"A devil of a wind, isn't it?"

"Yes," said I, "a terrific gale."

Indeed a storm coming from the west was sweeping Paris. It grappled everything in its path, stooping to the smallest details. Papers coming from who knows where and gathering none knows how coursed through the city. The trees shook as they bent, desperate and mad. Whistlings were born of dark places, while a sort of thunder rose from the roofs; windowpanes were bursting almost everywhere, giving out metallic and joyous sounds. Rage following madness gripped all things. The Seine grew choppy or spun about in whirls from minute to minute.

The wind beat unmercifully upon the buildings and lifted the dust and sand. It invaded the streets, driving before it all that offered resistance. Octave abandoned himself with evident pleasure to these huge movements of the air.

Then the wind began to flow like a great irresistible river.

Octave, as a small child might do, held his finger in the air after having sucked it, then walked into the storm. He went as fast as he was able, shouldering himself forward, head down—I followed as best I could, but I was out of breath.

All at once Octave seized my arm and bending toward me he cried:

"It won't rain, will it?"

I shook my head to say that I did not think so.

We walked for a long time in the night and in the wind, without meeting a living soul. I didn't know where we were going, but I kept on just the same, unable to resist Octave's headlong drive. I could fight against nothing except the formidable wind which blew ever harder and faster.

This chase seemed never to end and I did not think it ever would. We were drowned in the wind.

We crossed several bridges before arriving at Octave's shed, which I quickly recognized. This had been his goal. He gave me the key to hold, then after opening his door, he took it again. With his hand, as one might to a dog, he signaled me to be gone. Motionless, I looked at him but he started forward as if to frighten me. He waved his arms. I was incapable of moving, stunned by that constant whistling and beaten by the wind. Octave came up to me and demanded:

"Cigarette, please."

I searched through my pockets like a drunken man, offered him a pack. He took one, gave me back the rest. Then he ordered:

"Matches."

He seized the box I held out to him, then he gave me a rough shove to send me on my way.

The wind seized me in its turn and taking possession of me forced me to proceed. I had no longer the strength to resist and with shaky legs, I let myself go.

Like a carrier pigeon, I took the road along which we had come, but in the opposite direction, and when I turned to cross the bridge, I glanced about. Octave had disappeared.

While crossing the bridge, I implored help. The night was wild. But all at once a blaze shot up—like a flash of lightning, but continuous. Again I turned to look and saw, at the very spot where a moment or two before I had left Octave in accordance with his wish, a great flame which burst from the quay.

The wind drove it toward me. It continued to lick at the surroundings of Octave's shack after that had been devoured. It seemed to flow from that source and to spread like a blot. It ran; it leaped, struggling against the night. Then it redoubled on itself to become a ball of fire. There was in that gleam a joyous madness. In the space of a second I witnessed the metamorphoses of that flame. It became a fabulous beast, a cloud at dusk, red lace, a wound. Then it turned into a great circle, a circle formed by shapely hands linked together. Finally the flame concealed itself, to reappear still higher as a prancing horse.

It was too much for me. I felt like yelling, like shouting for help maybe, but I burst into a horrible laugh, as if something were ripped apart in me, when rain, a tremendous downpour, began to fall relentlessly. Buckets of water splashed upon the ground. Slowly the wind receded, hesitated, then died away.

I ran for shelter, a small box of a place used by chilly travelers waiting for the train. I was exhausted and lay flat on the ground. The rain was a tremendous song.

The swollen gutters swamped the highway and inundated the sidewalks.

For a long time I watched the great drops of rain falling, then I closed my eyes and slept.

I was awakened by an early morning traveler who smiled as he shook me. He took me for a drunk and was not altogether wrong. I got up, very much abashed, and with the flat of my hand began to brush my clothes.

"You just escaped it," said he, "as did we all. There was a fire near here last night on the other bank of the Seine. It's just by a miracle that the houses on this side the water didn't take fire, for the trees are scorched. Sparks must have crossed the Seine. The rain saved us."

As he talked, I regained my wits little by little. I walked to the site of the conflagration and saw a great blackened area, ravaged by the flames. Wooden houses, small Sunday restaurants, had been reduced to a handful of ashes.

I thought of Octave's grandiose project and of his destiny. Volpe would soon be saying: "He missed his chance."

Already the curious had begun to gather about the site of the "disaster," and ventured a few remarks:

"All Levallois might have burned."

"No, not a chance, the wind would have driven the flames in the direction of Neuilly."

"And . . ."

Each with the usual taste for misfortune tried to imagine a great disaster, but each came back to a little fire of no significance whatever.

Octave's latest experiments had not succeeded; an officer who had been searching through the ashes came back to say: "There must be someone dead in there, it smells like roast meat over by the little shed."

The news circulated and was distorted. I had nothing more to do, nothing more to hear, and nevertheless something, I don't know what, kept me in this place.

I think I wanted to know Octave's fate. I felt sure that he had wanted to take part in his "experiment" and that he had, in all probability, even sought to be the victim of it, but I wanted to be certain.

When that evening, after having watched the investigations of firemen for hours, I entered the café, all knew long since that Octave had planned to set fire to Paris. Volpe had suspected as much and had gone to his house to see what preparations he had made. Not finding Georgette, he had started looking for her and had instituted a search.

It was in vain.

Georgette had disappeared.

She did not come as upon other nights, strolling around Saint-Germain-l'Auxerrois or wandering in the Palais Royal.

Volpe himself set watch for her, the man in the slouch hat questioned the habitués. No one knew what had become of her. The very evening before she had been seen following her habit and custom.

CHAPTER THIRTEEN

For several days the rain continued to fall. Paris covered itself in a veil and a heat cut by gusts of cold wind took possession of the streets.

Three colors disputed the inundated city.

Sad tidings were current. One could almost see them floating in the moist air like butterflies. The sole refuge, once again, was the night.

Toward evening deliverance from servitude to the water and from automatic comings and goings seemed at hand. One no longer believed in repose, but one desired something else, something resembling joy, news.

I was on the watch for this news, I wished to know the final details of Octave's death, or to succeed in finding some trace of Georgette who in my eyes was now no more than a ragged woman. It seemed to me that at last poverty and anxiety for the morrow had vanquished her whom I had long thought stronger than the night.

Octave's ashes, which the police did not succeed in finding, I seemed to see in the yard, behind the burnt debris of the shed. A heavy odor spread to the borders of the street, but it was lost in all the smoke, the noises, and the evacuations from the factories of the neighborhood.

Octave was allowed to rot and the weeks poured their oblivion over him like so much sand. The supposed presence of this corpse allowed me to believe that Georgette, in some lost corner, was patiently waiting for the time to pass, smiling at her deliverance; she would chuckle, no doubt, concealed beneath the disguise of an honorable profession, on thinking of the peacefully passing days, of that tranquillity which had followed anxiety. She was conquered by her alibi. At least I believed that she could not live stripped of her habits. She was lost. Day had taken possession of her.

In the streets that formerly she had patrolled with such

astonishing regularity I could detect phosphorescent traces of her passage, which I thereupon labeled souvenirs. When I caught sight of a shadow in the rue Saint-Honoré or rue des Prêtres-Saint-Germain-l'Auxerrois, I could hardly keep from recognizing it. Sometimes also on coming across a couple entering some small, dingy, sad and dark hotel, it was she whom I saw push open the door.

She was no longer exactly night, but her shadow or the memory of her shadow was multiplied as reflections are multiplied.

During these walks I no longer beheld emotion rising suddenly before me. Women rotated, groups of them scattered right and left like flocks of birds. Not one of them knew how to light the street or to darken a passageway.

Each night Georgette drew off a little farther from the streets she had haunted. Then suddenly her image would burst forth as if to give me the lie. Time does not wipe out the tracks of those who have gone but is content to hide them from our sight. There remains either a scent or perhaps just some subtle difference in the atmosphere which brings them wholly to mind.

I continued to wander about Paris.

And I thought of all those who once upon a time had gathered about Georgette and who were still seeking her, like those who have suffered an amputation and still believe that the lost member is a part of themselves. Once upon a time. The irony of these words seemed suffocatingly heavy. Those men whom I had known craved to live but in the here and the now. By every means in their power they had always been at pains to abolish time. Verbaut the theorist, as was his custom, was ready to oppose this attitude, but Volpe would willingly have confessed that he knew nothing of patience, that his wishes had instantly to be realized.

And now all were watching the future and evoking the past.

It was not only regret for a being who had vanished that played such havoc with them, but the annoyance of a mystery too close at hand. If they had been able to seize the truth of Georgette's case by the throat, they would have been freed of a great weight. Certain of them would have been inclined to melancholy, others toward forgetfulness perhaps, Volpe would have sought someone else. But they knew nothing and they felt themselves dupes, dupes of themselves, dupes each of the other, dupes finally of all that they still took themselves to be.

I remembered what Volpe had said to me about Georgette, and his prophecy: "If she should disappear. . . ." Volpe had not only an interest in but also a certain sense of the future, a thing which at times gave some of his affirmations a tragic charm.

While they were on Georgette's trail, there was again some mention in the newspapers of the sailor, who came ever more rarely to this café which they called among themselves the *café bleu*. Driven by a feeling difficult to understand, which, however, has been observed in other cases, he had the strange idea of writing a letter to one of the large morning papers, which published his missive, with many reservations. Only those who knew a part of the truth were frightened by this useless audacity. Volpe could not get over his anger, looking upon it as a deliberate provocation. His rôle in this affair was becoming obscure and difficult to explain.

"A blowhard," said he, "like the rest. Always this desire to confess!"

One night, dragging his great sack as usual, the sailor entered the *café bleu*. Verbaut was sitting at a table in company with his friends. He still knew nothing of the sailor's crime and wondered at the presence of this person whom he considered a fool.

The sailor said to him simply: "I just saw Georgette."

Verbaut leaped up and demanded an explanation. Meanwhile Volpe came in. I was with him that night, for I also wanted the news.

The sailor was questioned minutely and related that, loitering about the various stations as was his habit, he thought he had seen Georgette, a traveling bag in her hand, walk into the waiting room, but he couldn't remember whether it had been the waiting room of the east or the north station.

Plied with questions, he ended by being not quite so certain; he insisted that he still believed it was Georgette who had disappeared in the crowd, but that he could no longer swear to it.

Verbaut, beside himself, asked for a description of her dress and seemed, he did not himself know why, to attach great importance to this fact: Did Georgette wear a veil or not?

That same night Verbaut, always methodical, proposed

that each of us should take it upon himself to watch a certain section of Paris. The man in the soft hat, Octave's friend, approved the proposal, which was finally adopted. Volpe alone remained skeptical of the results.

They cast lots for the different sections of Paris. I was charged with watching the neighborhood of the Parc Monceau.

I was convinced of the uselessness of such a chase for I felt certain that Georgette had left Paris. But when I raised this objection, it was received with bursts of laughter.

Georgette, in their eyes, was incapable of quitting Paris.

Toward the close of day I wandered about the railings of the Parc Monceau. The adjoining streets, gray, without shops, without cries, without passers-by, wakened but in the evening. From the long windows of the old-fashioned houses float songs and laughter, and the daughters of the landlords begin to repeat their do, re, mi's. In the morning one almost expects to see the bold fair ones of thirty years ago in baggy bloomers, traveling by bicycle to the porte Maillot. One can see them traversing the Parc Monceau, saluting the proud statues as they pass: Ambroise Thomas, beside an improved drinking fountain, thoughtfully studies

Guy de Maupassant from afar. The latter, more and more nervous despite his smile, refuses to be inveigled by the song of the fountain and the wiles of the lady. Can it be that this alluringly dressed woman will yield to despair and throw herself into the lake, where columns and ruins are ironically reflected?

All is gray in this park: the lake is of aluminum, the paths are sanded with dust, the trees covered with verdigris. The carriages go at a walk, so as not to frighten the sparrows; the nurse girls close their eyes.

I walked about this whimsicality enclosed in a railing and grasped the shadows of hopes as they flitted by. Often, frightened by my constant and unaccountable reappearances, the women would move out of my way. In this quarter dating from 1890, the prostitutes, too, have manners quite out-of-date. They flee to attract, they hum ditties to pass away the time, on the slightest provocation—for nothing at all—they begin to cry.

I was losing my time. The places and people I could see were only snares, vain reproaches. Georgette could not and would not have frequented these streets, this park, these boulevards, cold country of boredom.

Sometimes, at the close of night, I returned for news and was told of useless expeditions. Verbaut, as always, spoke of decisions to be made. He was the first to abandon these nocturnal meanderings. His task had been to watch the vicinity of the Gare Montparnasse and in the neighboring streets he had observed discouraging incidents.

The man in the soft hat had not lost his time watching the Panthéon, for he simply set about questioning the women. But never a serious clue did we get.

One of them, Blin, had for a long time followed the sailor whom he suspected of knowing something and of betraying the gang. He related with irritating exactitude all the incidents of his pursuit. The sailor had walked about Paris in zigzags, sleeping now in a Montrouge hotel, now at Grenelle, always being most careful not to remain two consecutive nights under the same roof.

Beyond that he seemed not to fear our company and I often saw him come to borrow money of Volpe.

Obviously he enjoyed this vagrant life and thought no more of giving himself up. His silent presence annoyed most of his companions.

After having finished smoking a cigarette, he would smile with a distant air as if all the angry looks he encountered amused him enormously. One day near the café, he met his former mistress, her for whom he had committed murder. He pretended he no longer wished to see her, but nevertheless he did not avoid her. He took her to the café with him and they awaited Volpe, who was late in making his appearance.

Now and then the sailor spoke in a low voice to this Marie who, understanding little by little the plot of which she had been the victim, fell into a sort of melancholy. She felt herself condemned in the eyes of all, since she had at first put up a fight, only to end by yielding.

When Volpe arrived, she concealed herself behind the sailor, who as always remained undisturbed. When he had addressed his petition to Volpe and when, according to his habit, this latter had given him a bank note, he left without further ceremony, accompanied by Marie.

The next day we learned that Marie and the sailor, under the eyes of Blin, had quitted Paris, probably without expecting to return. Hearing of this flight from the windbag, Volpe contented himself with shrugging his shoulders. The hunt had not ceased but, whereas at the start all had rivaled one another in ardor and vigilance, at the end of several nights evident signs of weariness became apparent. Verbaut, the most determined at the start, seemed the most disgusted and the most fagged. Seeing him spent, Volpe smiled with satisfaction.

One night shortly thereafter, unable to do more, Verbaut suggested holding a meeting the next day, at which, declared he, definite decisions would have to be made.

Volpe made no objection and a rendezvous was set for a café near the place de la Nation.

CHAPTER FOURTEEN

Volpe was waiting for me outside the café.

Before entering he advised me to take a look in through the window.

"But I know them all more or less," I told him.

"You hardly know them at all," replied he.

Nevertheless I recognized sitting around the group's favorite table a number of guests that were affecting the appearance of conspirators. There were present: Verbaut; Blin, elegant as always; then he whom they called Billie the Clown.

"Look at my friends," said Volpe—with a malicious

laugh! "I'm riding easy; tonight they are forced to come to some decision. They don't know what, but they're up against it. They're going to talk, then you'll see. They're waiting for you. You are the spectator and they can't resist the pleasure of astonishing you."

"I know Verbaut, I know . . ."

"You don't know them at all," interrupted Volpe with his customary harshness. "But I know them. I knew Verbaut when he was still a druggist's apprentice, and he'd come to me to place a bet. He was smiling and sweet, making himself pleasant, always without a cent in his pocket, but a fine talker. Ah, yes! as far as that goes, he talks and shouts ravishingly, and Boulet, the one they call Billie the Clown, he's the son of a baker. Always in hot water. A famous thief. His mother let him do anything he pleased, up to the day the boss saw him dipping into the cash drawer and very properly kicked him out. The father was a little hard and the other prefers not to see him again.

"As to Blin, how easy it is to size him up, he is a former schoolmaster. He thinks he knows everything, quite sincerely, you understand. When he twists his little moustache and says: 'Listen to me . . .' everything may contradict him, but there is no way to keep him from talking."

Volpe was revenging himself for I don't know what. He seemed happy to be able to say, while looking at what he called "those young men," all that he had in mind. He had an aggressive look.

But, while we were still looking through the windows of the café at those who were waiting inside, we could not help sharing, so contagious was it, the anxiety which filled them. I knew that this anxiety had been created out of whole cloth, but this made little difference.

We entered the café and the discussion began at once. What was said that evening, that night, concerning Georgette? It was not a question of the life of a person, but of life in general. The debate rose and fell. Each added his bit and words were thrown about recklessly. Nothing was arrived at. The hours, however, slipped rapidly by under Volpe's smile. Stupid and sad, it was! The shadows which people Paris by night, those impatient shadows awaited the daily signal in vain. They were hid in small lights which turn softly like clocks.

The gallop of three in the morning, the gallop of the cavalry of black thought, could not be heard. And in the too pale sky were vanishing the last clouds, heritors of day. One of us said: The white hour has come. But his neighbor replied: It is scarcely propitious—and as if to support the last speaker, the door slammed, which is indisputably a bad omen.

Blin stood up and took the floor: "Come now, let's weigh these things, think of all the circumstances, of the fickleness and treasons of the night. . . ."

He wanted to continue, but one of us signaled him to stop. Then for the first time you could hear the loud noise of early morning: a metallic clatter, dull thuds, whistlings, the screeching of wheels.

That night had come to an end.

It was time.

One by one eyes became dim. Sleep came upon us visibly, and on the resurrected silence a deeper silence was imposed. All this in expectation of daylight, as if it were the end of the world. Despair cautiously drew nearer.

Despair is cloaked most of the time in white. His face is at times that of a woman and at times that of an old man. His gait is as deliberate as his gestures. You know he will never fly into a temper. He never conceals his tenderness and yet when he draws near, a sharp perfume spreads and penetrates, a perfume that often one uses alcohol to overcome. He is the enemy of fear, his favorite servant is courage, his mistress is audacity.

The pilgrims of this corner café could not pride themselves on this presence. They were content to fold their hands and to look at each other. They knew that morning, color of fog, would see a final decision and that it would be something unexpected.

Visibly they all lacked courage and their wills had melted like sugar. Their hands hung at their sides, their cigarettes were going out and they permitted despair to come sit at their table.

Of course, I, too, knew that there was nothing more to do, but I still hoped.

My eyes rested on Volpe, the man with the big head and swollen lips. He was very pale and seemed ill at ease in his black clothes. One felt that he would have wished to speak, to utter words, no matter what so long as they were positive, and to move his big hands which now slept beneath the table.

Verbaut nervously pulled on a cigarette as hard as he could, then took it from his mouth to flick off the ash. That office finished, his hand again drowsed off.

Blin, his neighbor, tried hard to smile, but he seemed above all to be occupied with his cuffs which were giving him no rest. In this struggle he acknowledged himself beaten. From time to time, but mostly to save his face, he wrote a phrase on the sheet of white paper he had very ostentatiously placed before him. The others expected much of these silent two, who would have preferred an explosion to this silence which sat in judgment.

Billie the Clown, the smallest, sitting at the end of the table, was now pocketing the cigarettes which his neighbor had negligently left out.

The struggle against time continued.

L'alcool bleu passa.

Blin, seizing his courage in both hands, got up and said: "There are various degrees of doubt just as there are progressive stages of insanity. You make me laugh. Let one of you throw the first stone, I'll fling it back. My position today permits me to face these obligations of which I myself have fixed the value. I demand, I DEMAND. . . ." The words—empty, useless, out-of-date—flowed until he was breathless. Verbaut was pained by the racket. He alone, perhaps, was aware that once again it was a question of another matter. But he abandoned himself to the stimulation of fear and the game. There was not yet fear enough and perhaps he would have been satisfied if the ceiling had suddenly crashed upon their heads. Instead of that someone rapped with his fingers on the windowpane. It was the manager of the café, who asked permission to call to our attention that the café was closing its doors and that we must vacate as quickly as possible.

Hardly had he finished his little speech when each arose, determined to bring this discussion to an end. Already several were extending their hands to take leave, but Verbaut stood still. His face was pale and from a distance one might have taken him for a hangman.

"I don't understand it that way. This thing's got to be finished. I expect you all, all, understand me, to meet me within an hour at my house and I hold any man who doesn't come to be the lowest of the low."

Several protested, but after that evening when the oppressive silence had weighed more than reason, words and insults carried an invincible power.

Morning and the cold had assailed Paris and only several street lamps, still burning, detained the night.

We hailed taxis which carried us at top speed through the deserted streets to the porte de Versailles.

In a small street adjoining the boulevard Victor, a massive house, now almost superannuated, served Verbaut as a den.

Discussion began again in a somber little room on the same level as the street, as soon as the band was complete. Volpe had seated himself near the door, smoking a fat cigar. He seemed to have come for the purpose of defying these men who were gathered in a pack. But Volpe was no longer the same. He mistrusted himself. The disappearance of Octave, then Georgette, had broken the chain which he held so firmly and which had helped him to manage "all his world," to threaten those who dared to oppose him.

Having permitted a part of his power to escape rendered him weak in his own eyes. He tried by bravado and habit to appear the same, but he was conscious that to all of them he had become just a man like anyone else. Volpe, because of his vanity, on reentering the ranks presented a poor figure there.

Verbaut took advantage of this new weakness and thrust ever shrewder questions at Volpe, going into the past and trying to push him to the wall. This apparent triumph stressed Verbaut's ready cruelty. He looked at Volpe evilly, as if he were at last revenging himself for the ascendency this man had in times past exercised over him.

However, the anxiety grew ever stronger. And I saw it swell. A sort of panic had seized everyone. They were really in despair, all, all without exception. By a strange and subtle phenomenon, all saw in this disappearance a direct accusation and each feared the reproaches which they all addressed to themselves. From a cause unknown to me, their lives were at stake.

It was at once ridiculous and tragic.

It was partially that they feared the revelations Georgette could make, but above all it was because they had placed a finger on their weakness. Let one single person suddenly fail to answer the call and they no longer believed in the course of the universe.

The reality of death was uppermost in all their hearts. Adventure, which had tempted these spirits, had become a trap and here they were turning and twisting to escape this reality which pressed upon them from all sides. This reality seemed to have the strength and the depth of the sea. Had one of them suddenly been able to laugh or even to smile, it would have vanished. They could only talk and one felt that each word fell from them as if tolling the hours, that each word told them only of the flight of time. Their pride lay before them, at their feet.

Day was approaching. Through the big window which occupied all the free wall space, one could gradually make out roofs, chimneys, long walls, the little street, the trees of the boulevard—Paris. The whole city was coming to life, and we were on our way, we believed we were on our way, to meet her. Someone knocked on the door.

That was too much. We all stopped talking immediately. Another knock.

"Come in," said Volpe.

And Georgette entered. The cold and the morning followed her.

"Is it you?" someone ventured.

"It is I," answered she, and smiled.

Paris was before our eyes.

We had no one else to wait for.

Now there was a great burst of flame, a piece of red lace, a wound. Not far from there a house had taken fire and again I saw the circle of joined hands.

We listened, without saying a word. On the threshold of the door which she had left open, Georgette waited. The smoke neared us along with the tumult of the firemen.

Volpe ran to see and one by one we followed him. At the porte de Versailles I saw a slow column of men, women, and beasts who were entering Paris.

The day and the night began again their round.

THE END

AFTERWORD

✳

WILLIAM CARLOS WILLIAMS IN PARIS
BY DAY AND BY NIGHT
BY
PHILIPPE SOUPAULT

I think William Carlos Williams was happy during his stay
in Paris. I often walked around with him in the streets of
the capital. He looked at the shops with amazement, but
especially at the women and men who like to stroll along
the boulevards. We often sat down at outdoor cafés and
watched the passers-by passing by. He sat down and set
about asking me questions on the manners and morals of
the residents of the different neighborhoods of Paris, the
variety of which pleased him. "Such traveling!" he said.
Because he was surprised by the monuments haunted by the

tourists. The fact is that Williams was not a tourist. He was a spectator.

He preferred his solitary strolls to the "exiled" Americans' get-togethers and the dinners put together by Bob McAlmon. I think he even refused to go back to Gertrude Stein's after a first visit. I had the impression that he wanted to be more Parisian than his numerous compatriots in Montparnasse.

I had the great pleasure of accompanying him at night in the deserted streets and on the quays along the Seine. Sometimes we sat down on a bench to admire the moonlight and the vagabonds who preferred night to the light of day. For reasons he easily guessed.

I think it was the memory of these nocturnal wanderings that made him decide to accept translating my "testimony," incorrectly subtitled "novel," *Last Nights of Paris*. Which for me was a great joy. I was one of the few Europeans (or Americans) who knew that Williams was a great, a very great poet and an admirable writer of incomparable lucidity and even of incurable modesty. He never talked about what he had written or what he wanted to write. He was more interested in his friends' projects. One day he made it known that he wanted to meet James Joyce, who at that time was working on *Finnegans Wake*. The two writers shook hands but said nothing. I was told, though never by Williams, that he had momentarily considered moving to Paris to practice medicine. It's possible, but I doubt it.

In fact I had the impression that at the end of his European visit Williams was in a hurry to get back to the United States, to his patients and his work table. But, as he has written, he had retained pleasant memories of our walks in Paris, which he evoked in translating, with his mother, *Last Nights of Paris*.

And after reading his translation I congratulated him, because he had done an admirable job of describing the atmosphere of the Parisian nights. In his autobiography, I found the testimony of our friendship, that of a great American poet and a young, nonconformist French poet.

translated by Ron Padgett